# KIERKEGAARD'S WAY
# TO THE TRUTH

# KIERKEGAARD'S WAY TO THE TRUTH

*An Introduction to the Authorship of*
**SØREN KIERKEGAARD**

*By Gregor Malantschuk*

*Translated from the Danish by*
MARY MICHELSEN

Augsburg Publishing House
Minneapolis, Minnesota

KIERKEGAARD'S WAY TO THE TRUTH

This volume is an English version of the Danish book *Indførelse i Søren Kierkegaards forfatterskab,* published by Munksgaard, Copenhagen, with two additional chapters translated from the theological journal *Dansk Teologisk Tidsskrift,* published by Gads Verlag, Copenhagen: "Frihedens Dialektik hos Søren Kierkegaard" and "Problemer omkring Selvet og Udødeligheden i Søren Kierkegaards Forfatterskab."

Manufactured in the United States of America

To
Peter Zilinski
with gratitude

# *Foreword*

The best approach to any thinker, and especially to Kierkegaard, is through his writings. Conceivably an exception might be made for a "philosophers' philosopher." This, however, is hardly the case with Kierkegaard, inasmuch as he intended to present his thought and to write in such a way that the reader would as a man become involved in the issues. The aim of his "indirect communication" was to make the author a vanishing point and to avoid direct presentation of a system of argument and conclusions, not because of the unimportance of decisive thought, but because of the primary importance of the reader's own decisive thought. The writings themselves were to be primarily occasions and not deliverances.

The nature and intention of the authorship, therefore, relegates secondary works about the authorship, and certainly those about the author, to a distinctly secondary role, at least second or third in the order of time. What, then, about secondary works which more ostensibly have the purpose of being an introduction to Kierkegaard's writings? Is there any place at all for them, if the best introduction is through the works themselves?

My answer, after affirming this best way, is that there is a place
for a good introduction—an introduction which does introduce
one to the works and not to "the man behind the works" or to
another author's understanding or misunderstanding of the
works and his ruminations thereabout. There have been more
than enough of such short-circuiting introductions. The very
presence of diversionary introductions makes a proper introduction valuable, and hopefully Gresham's Law is not operative
in this realm as in the realm of good and bad money.

Some potential readers of Kierkegaard's works, confronted
by the formidable array of writings in the authorship and not
satisfied with secondary substitutes, may wonder where one
should begin. The reading of Kierkegaard's works in the order
of publication, with the built-in dialectic, is not now the practical requirement it originally was, inasmuch as we have all
(almost all) the authorship available simultaneously. One
therefore is likely to read what is at hand or what has somehow
been mentioned and to take this as a sample of the whole. Imagine beginning with "The Diary of a Seducer" and considering
this as representative! This itself would be a seduction. To
know where and how to begin reading Kierkegaard calls for at
least some guidance concerning the authorship, an elementary
introduction to avoid confusion of part and whole. Such geo-
graphical intelligence would be a good introduction.

The present small volume is a good introduction simply because it does introduce—it introduces one to *Kierkegaard's*
thought rather than to some other writing and to some other
writer using Kierkegaard as a point of departure. This does not
mean the claim of immaculate objectivity for any writer—or
reader—but it does mean a proper center of gravity. This does
not mean a depreciation of historical and critical studies, but

it does mean that such studies are no substitute for the authorship and thought which such studies presuppose. Kierkegaard
wrote about those who want to "go beyond" Heraclitus, beyond
Socrates, beyond Descartes, beyond Abraham, beyond Christianity—without having understood and appropriated these
supposedly vanishing positions. Gregor Malantschuk in this
volume does not indulge in the luxury of loftily introducing
Kierkegaard from a point beyond, but instead he does introduce one to *Kierkegaard's* works.

Besides knowing his subject and pointing a reader to that
subject from within its own substance, Dr. Malantschuk avoids
confusing that subject with other subjects or with the author
of that subject. It is particularly easy to commit the genetic
fallacy with regard to an existential thinker and thereby to present biographical, psychological, and personal studies rather
than to point to the thought and the works. Such approaches
may at times illuminate the thought; nevertheless, although
they are not the thought and cannot "explain" or give grounds
of evaluation, they tend to eliminate the thought. Biography
is a legitimate sphere of interest, but it ought not be equated
with that which reminds us that the individual, the author,
ever lived at all. This compact *Introduction,* although making
occasional illuminating use of personal history, does introduce
the reader to Kierkegaard's *works* and keeps the author in the
background, just as Kierkegaard meant him to be.

In addition, this little book has the merit of introducing *the
reader* to Kierkegaard's works. Professor Billeskov Jansen of
Copenhagen has written that Dr. Malantschuk has produced a
"model of popular scholarship," that he has the ability to
"speak with the learned and to speak popularly with those who
require it." This volume does not pamper the reader; yet it is

for any concerned, intelligent ordinary man. It represents what Kierkegaard called "going there where a man is" if one would lead him somewhere—or introduce him to something. Chapters V and VI on the self and on freedom are of another kind, in that they may be more fruitful after some reading in the works themselves or may be a more congenial introduction for those who can begin bare-handed with core issues.

Because Dr. Malantschuk, one of the most penetrating and most modest students of Kierkegaard in Scandinavia today, has written such an introduction and Mary Michelsen has successfully brought it into English, Edna Hong and I are happy to have had the opportunity of seeing it through the press for a new reading audience (besides Danish, Dutch, and Portuguese). Acknowledgment is gratefully made to Munksgaards Forlag for copyright permission, to The Rask-Ørsted Fund for underwriting the translating, and to the editorial staff of Augsburg Publishing House for many things of the *sine qua non* variety.

HOWARD V. HONG

St. Olaf College
December 1, 1962

# *Preface*

During the autumn of 1951 I delivered four lectures to the
Søren Kierkegaard Society in Copenhagen under the title, "An
Introduction to the Works of Søren Kierkegaard." In the hope
that this introduction may appeal to a larger circle, these lectures are now being published.

In addition to giving an insight into the works of Søren
Kierkegaard, I had the following aims in these lectures:

First, I wanted to point out Kierkegaard's significance for
the spiritual conflicts of the present time as well as for those
of the future.

Second, by reviewing Kierkegaard's works, I sought to
demonstrate his claim that his authorship is developed in progressive stages. Kierkegaard writes about this in the preface
to "Two Sermons for Good Friday Communion (1851)," the
work that concludes his description of the stages in human life,
just before he enters into a polemical and provocative indict-
ment of the contemporary age.

The second aim led to the third, which was to demonstrate
the wonderful design working through the authorship, a design

9

which Kierkegaard naturally did not at first completely understand, but which, when he at last fully comprehended it, he gratefully attributed to "the Governing Power."

This brief summary of the works of Søren Kierkegaard may illuminate his methods of dealing with the different themes of his authorship.

I have tried to make this introduction simple and easy to understand, without, however, erasing the possibility of individual thought.

GREGOR MALANTSCHUK

Copenhagen
October, 1952

EDITOR'S NOTE: Since the publication in Denmark, Holland, and Brazil of *Introduction to the Works of Søren Kierkegaard,* two articles by Dr. Malantschuk pertaining to aspects of Kierkegaard's authorship crucial to the modern dilemma have appeared in a Danish theological journal. Augsburg Publishing House considers them of such significance that it includes them in this English edition of Dr. Malantschuk's book.

# Contents

                                                            Page

   I.  The Age of Disintegration ....................................   13

  II.  The Aesthetic Stage ...............................................   23

 III.  The Ethical Stage .................................................   40

  IV.  The Religious Stage.............................................   52

   V.  The Problems of the Self and Immortality............   79

  VI.  The Dialectic of Freedom ...................................   97

 VII.  The Dialectic of Communication ...........................   114


       Bibliography and Notes ........................................   121

# I. *The Age of Disintegration*

Interest in the works of Søren Kierkegaard is steadily increasing, and the future will demonstrate that this is not merely a current craze. About a century elapsed before this thinker met with any real attention. Now that he is discovered, he will exert more and more influence because no one has understood more deeply than he the central issues in the future struggle and strife of man. Kierkegaard was conscious of the fact that he was inaugurating a turning point in man's thinking and orientation. He declares that he has related himself properly to "the shift which will take place and which will become history's future."[1] His anticipation of being useful to the future is therefore understandable. Kierkegaard was one of the first to perceive that his own age as well as the coming one was the "age of disintegration,"[2] and he understood it as his task to find that truth which alone might rescue man from spiritual destruction.

The outstanding characteristic of the age of disintegration, says Kierkegaard, is that in such an age nothing is absolutely solid. No longer does man have an absolute standard by which he may order his life. Belief in eternal values is replaced by the leveling of all values. But without belief in something eternal, man gives himself over to annihilation.

The spiritual condition of the age of disintegration has been developing for a long time. Christianity, after an initial hard struggle with the pagan world, succeeded in making the eternal values respected and in demonstrating to man the purpose of life. For generations and centuries after this the truths of Christianity stood unshakably firm, but gradually influences developed that turned man away from Christian truth and advanced modern paganism.

Christianity pointed out to man his limitations and his sin. It demanded obedience and belief. But modern man wants to be his own master and would rather not acknowledge a limit to his knowledge and powers. Natural science and modern philosophy have done their best to further this development. The Christian understanding that man can be related to the eternal truths only through faith is now replaced by human attempts to attain the whole truth through man's own endeavor. Man will not acknowledge other truths than those attained through observation and logic.

These trends, gradually coming to the fore ever since the Renaissance, attained their philosophical culmination in Hegel. This thinker consistently develops the view that man in himself —i.e., in his reason—possesses the source of all truth, and that thinking, with its strictly logical method, is able to fathom the truth about God, the world, and man. According to Hegel man is God's equal, for man's range of knowledge coincides with that of God.

There is no room left in Hegel for faith in the Christian sense of the word, for Hegel will not acknowledge any limit to

man's rational understanding. Reason, then, will forge to the front, and faith, which under different forms has maintained the lead from the beginning of Christianity until now, must drop back, defeated by this modern wisdom.

Even worse than this, Hegel tries to destroy the Christian concept of a transcendental world. Hegel's idea of God is completely bound up with this world. It is perfectly consistent, therefore, for Hegel to maintain that the concept of God attains its highest manifestation in the moral structure of the state.

From an ethical point of view, Hegel's philosophy—as Kierkegaard demonstrates—is not a progression but a regression to a type of paganism which existed prior to the time of Socrates. Pagan Socrates' outlook went beyond the much acclaimed views of Hegel. Socrates believed in a higher order of things than the state, and he tried to actualize this conviction in his life.\* Hegel, with his concept of the state as the highest entity, signals man's flight away from the eternal. Thus Hegel's philosophy creates the theoretical basis for the deification of the state and temporal life, just as by exalting the state as supreme it cuts man off from faith in a transcendent world.

There is deep irony in the fact that Hegel, who spoke so much of the absolute, actually laid the groundwork through his philosophy for the modern relativizing of values. They are not to be congratulated—those men of the church who failed to see the ominous consequences of Hegel's philosophy

---

\*Hegel's denial of a transcendent reality provokes Kierkegaard's assertion that Hegel's philosophy "has no ethics" (*Pap.* VII B 235, pp. 162 and 214, and *S.V.* VI, p. 218; Stages on Life's Way, p. 210; VII, p. 98; Postscript, p. 108). Kierkegaard believes that the possibility for an ethical orientation is closely bound to faith in a transcendent reality. Among other statements about Hegel, Kierkegaard declares (*S.V.*, VII, p. 438; Postscript, p. 450.): "The desperate attempt of Hegel's decadent ethics to make the state the ultimate form of the ethical is a highly unethical attempt to eliminate the individual, an unethical flight from the category of individuality into the category of the age or generation."

and even believed that it might help put some starch into Christianity!

Kierkegaard quickly perceives the dangerous tendencies in this modern development which Hegel and the new natural sciences introduced. He understands that these views are an attack on the Eternal. They will deprive man of his belief in the Eternal and will downgrade him to a merely temporal creature. By surrendering to these modern tendencies man will move toward his spiritual destruction.

Kierkegaard stands squarely in the middle of this dangerous situation. He describes graphically how he feels after having discovered the peril. He feels "like a spider who after the last house-cleaning manages to live his wretched life in a hidden corner while in anguish he feels within himself the impending storm."[3] In one of the last notes in his *Journal* Kierkegaard speaks even more to the point of the steadily approaching danger. He compares himself to a passenger on a sailing vessel where all are making merry while a storm is gathering. He discovers "the ominous white spot on the horizon" and tries to warn against the threatening storm. He writes:

> The white spot is on the horizon. There it is. A terrible storm is brewing. But no one sees the white spot or has any inkling of what it might mean. But no (this would not be the most terrible situation either), no, there is one person who sees it and knows what it means— but he is a passenger. He has no authority on the ship, can take no action. . . . The fact that in Christendom there is visible on the horizon a white speck which means that a storm is threatening—this I knew; but, alas, I was and am only a passenger![4]

Because of his Christian upbringing and the experiences of his youth, Kierkegaard at a very early age was stirred by this dangerous situation and the modern confusion to look for something solid — an Archimedean point — which might endure through the storm and in life and in death. In a note in his *Journal* from Gilleleje in 1835 the earnestness of his decision to find the truth at any cost is apparent. He writes: "The main thing is that I understand my purpose in life and that I see what God really wants *me* to do. My main concern is to find a truth which is truth *for me*, that I find *the idea for which I will live and die.*"[5]

It could not be anything but the old Christianity which in the following difficult years of struggle for Kierkegaard manifests itself as the eternally fast point. After he himself has been captured and conquered by Christianity, he regards it as his particular calling to draw the attention of men to Christianity as the only way out of the anxiety and hopelessness of the modern age. He believes that he has been given good talents for this task—especially a lively imagination and a superb capacity for reflection. With the aid of his imagination he can live himself into other men's points of view and understand them. Reflection and a scrupulously logical mind help him to be incorruptible and consistent in his seeking for and communicating of truth.

Equipped with these gifts, and with Christianity as his starting point, Kierkegaard sets himself to the task of understanding human life in all its stages and in all its relationships, in order that through this understanding it may become clear to him how man may be helped to the truth again. Kierkegaard attempts to find a link and a line of development in all the contradictory possibilities of human life. He knows that one can help another human being only if he fully understands the whole of human life.

In the first volumes of the *Journals* we can follow closely Kierkegaard's struggle to fathom man's being and to unite the different manifestations of human life under a definite and

coherent view. In spite of the immensity of the task, Kierkegaard's aim is less presumptuous than Hegel's. Hegel intended
to explain both God and man in his philosophy. Kierkegaard is
content with trying to find his bearings in human existence and,
contrary to Hegel, to sketch the boundary of human knowledge.

A study of Kierkegaard's reading also shows that his special
interest is man in his existence. He supplements his theological,
philosophical, and aesthetic studies by reading those works and
authors with the greatest promise of yielding the best and most
reliable illumination of man. Only the most important themes
of his ardent reading will be mentioned here.

Kierkegaard dives into the world of mythology, fairy tales,
and saga. Here he acquires his insight into the primitive and
childlike life of the human soul.

Through his study of the Greeks and their philosophy Kierkegaard learns how man began consciously and critically to understand and to shape his existence and to build systematic knowledge on the basis of logical principles. He is especially attracted
by the personality of Socrates, whom he comes to regard as the
best representative of human understanding and action within
paganism.

From the church fathers and the Christian mystics Kierkegaard acquires an insight into the willingness with which a
human being can make sacrifices in order to come in contact
with the Eternal.

Kierkegaard becomes very engrossed in the study of Don
Juan, Faust, and the Wandering Jew, and comes to see them as
symbols of the protest and revolt of man's emotions, mind, and
will against Christianity. He also reads Shakespeare intensively
and is richly rewarded with a fine psychological insight into the
different types and characters of human life.

In the German philosopher Hamann, Kierkegaard finds an honest man's confession of how little a man can achieve by himself. The writings of Hamann also help him perceive more clearly the difference between human knowledge and the revealed truth.

Kierkegaard is also quite occupied by the German romantic poets—such as Schlegel, Tieck, and Hoffmann. The damaging influences of this literary movement have no small part in calling his attention to the fact that "the age of disintegration" has arrived.

Kierkegaard's most significant reading, however, comes to be the Bible, the book that portrays the advent of God and how God casts man into the most earnest decision of his existence. With his creative imagination Kierkegaard enters into all the human experiences and adventures he meets in this reading. He relives them and tries by consistent and logical reasoning to find a coherence in them. He finally comes to believe that he has succeeded in finding the laws and directions along which man's existence moves. He encompasses this total view of human life in his theory of the stages.

Kierkegaard is fully convinced that the theory of the stages embraces all the possibilities of human existence. He expresses this in the following note in his diary: "My abiding service in literature will be to have stated the decisive determinants of the whole existential range of life with a dialectical acuteness and primitivity not to be found in any other literature, as far as I know—and I have not had any books to guide me."[6]

Anyone who has seriously studied the basic thinking of the theory of the stages must admit in any case that it is the first time in the history of man that a view of man has been formulated in which all the aspects and all the possibilities of human life have been consistently worked together in a developmental sequence. All attempts in this direction before Kierkegaard are only fragmentary. The theory of the stages also helps Kierkegaard to construct the unique Kierkegaardian anthropology which still awaits full and adequate presentation.

For reasons which will be touched upon later, Kierkegaard does not give a coherent and readily explicit survey of the theory of the stages, yet it is this view which forms the basis of his whole authorship.

Kierkegaard predicates three stages of human life: the aesthetic, the ethical, and the religious. These stages should be spacious enough to encompass all the levels of the life of man in his journey through the world. Before going into a study of the separate stages, we must first examine what Kierkegaard uses as a basis for the theory itself.

An examination of the structure of the stages shows that Kierkegaard builds his whole theory on a very simple and clear presupposition—that man is a synthesis of two completely different qualities. Kierkegaard designates these two universal qualities, the components of every human being, by such terms as time and eternity, the finite and the infinite, body (and soul) and spirit, necessity and freedom, etc. These coupled terms all say the same thing—that man's being consists of two antithetical qualities. It would, however, go beyond the purpose of this short introduction to demonstrate how these coupled terms are only the different visual angles from which man as a synthesis can be regarded.

Kierkegaard derived his understanding of man as a composite of two completely different qualities from Christianity. It is certainly true that paganism also had an intimation of man as a double being, but Christianity is the first to express clearly that man is of flesh and of spirit, which are absolutely antithetic.

For the sake of simplicity and clarity, the most intelligible pair of terms—man as a synthesis of the temporal and the Eternal—will be scrutinized for the consequences this composite implies.

We discover first of all something quite obvious to Kierkegaard—that one of the elements of the synthesis must be of greater value than the other. The Eternal must be higher than the temporal, the spirit higher than body and soul, and so on. Secondly, it follows that when the two components stand in the right relationship to each other, the higher component must be the dominant one. Thirdly, because of the qualitative difference between the two components, man is faced at the outset with the task in existence of relating the two factors in the right manner.

Kierkegaard tries to include all the possibilities and contradictions of human life under this formulation: man is a synthesis. Out of this grows his theory of the stages, which is only a historical cloak for the synthesis and a corroboration of its truth. By reflecting on the different possibilities over against which the components of the synthesis place a man, we get in abridged perspective a glimpse of the whole structure of the stages.

Briefly stated, rooted in this synthesis, the following basic positions are open to a man's choosing. He may live exclusively in the visible, temporal world. This constitutes the aesthetic stage. He may seek the Eternal, or when the Eternal meets him he may accept the Eternal, and in either event he may try to relate the two components of the synthesis (the temporal and the Eternal). This constitutes the transition from the aesthetic to the ethical stage and, beyond this, to the religious stage. In the last stage there is always the dangerous possibility that a man knows about the Eternal but this knowledge has no meaning for his human existence, and he lives in despair over the disrelationship of the two components of the synthesis.

The theory of the stages, which is the basis of Søren Kierkegaard's whole authorship, is constructed on the premise that man is a synthesis of two different qualities. It is the possibility of using the premise of the synthesis in an amplified form—as in the theory of the stages—which gives Kierkegaard the consistency and accuracy characteristic of his thinking.

Following this enunciation of the principal feature of the authorship, it is time for a closer inspection of the separate stages in relationship to both components of the synthesis. To simplify the orientation, each stage with its various levels will be treated separately.

# II. *The Aesthetic Stage*

Kierkegaard proceeds from the scriptural doctrine that man was created a synthesis of the temporal and the Eternal and that the two components of this synthesis originally stood in the right relationship to each other. Man was obedient to the Eternal and lived in a state of innocence without knowledge of good and evil.

Since innocence as yet lacks the possibility of consciously discerning between good and evil, it follows that "innocence is ignorance. In his innocence man is not qualified as spirit but as soul in immediate union with his natural condition. Spirit is dreaming in man."[7]

But already the Eternal in man (spirit) is beginning to form itself poetically. "Dreamingly spirit projects its own reality,"[8] but this "dreaming of spirit,"[9] seen from a mature, spiritual point of view, is "nothing." Man himself creates this "nothing" and is attracted and intimidated by this his own creation. Kierkegaard more closely describes this ambiguous double position in man's relationship to "nothing" as "a *sympathetic antipathy* and an *antipathetic sympathy.*"[10] He believes it is best expressed by the term *angst* (*anxiety,* translated *dread* in present English version).

From now on anxiety does not mean the same as fear, which always refers to something particular and finite, but anxiety declares that man has the element of the Eternal within him. Without this Eternal element in man anxiety is impossible.

In his original condition man also possessed what Kierkegaard calls "the alarming possibility of *being able.*"[11] Man could choose to disobey the Eternal.

In his rather difficult book, *The Concept of Anxiety (Dread),* from which five passages have just been quoted, Kierkegaard describes how man detaches himself from the Eternal and how human history begins with the consequences of original sin.

Man clutches at the temporal but can never quite free himself from the other element of the synthesis—the Eternal. If man could do so, he would become an animal. The condition of fallen man continues to be anxiety since man must continually be related to the Eternal. We see, therefore, how pagan man creates his own religious objects and idols, about which he is then anxious. But here, too, the object of anxiety is "nothing," even if this "nothing" assumes tremendous proportions in future historical development.

Pagan man also is anxious about fate. This anxiety is easy enough to understand. In his search for the Eternal, pagan man meets at the extreme frontier a power to which both gods and men must submit. This power is Fate. Man wishes to be on good terms with Fate, but at the same time he is apprehensive of Fate. Anxiety is an apt description of this condition. The gods, who also make their demands on pagan man, as well as Fate, are both "nothing," something which man himself creates

because of the Eternal element in the synthesis and which he
thereafter is anxious about.*

At this point in man's development there is possibility only
for an aesthetic outlook because, as stated, the most important
element of the synthesis, the Eternal, is expressed only negatively as "the nothing of anxiety." Referring to this situation,
Kierkegaard says in *Concluding Unscientific Postscript:* "The
existence-sphere in paganism is essentially an aesthetic one."[12]
The Eternal in the form of the ethical has not yet appeared.
Man as yet knows no eternal demands. Man's whole sphere of
interest does not extend beyond the borders of the temporal, or,
in Kierkegaard's mode of expression, man still exists in the
domain of morality, which ranks lower than the essentially
ethical. Man's highest achievements in the realm of morality
will consist in a sacrifice for the sake of the community. *Fear
and Trembling* cites as examples of man's highest efforts on this
level such names as Agamemnon, Jephthah, and Brutus, all of
whom consider the welfare of the community to be superior
to their own interests.[13] Paganism culminates in the idea of state
and community. There are no higher laws, as yet, than those of
social morality and of the state. At this level the religious life
exists only as human imaginings and as anxiety over "nothing."

The aesthetic changes its character and loses its dominant
role when the Eternal makes its appearance as the ethical demand upon man. This happens twice in human history—in
paganism with Socrates and in Jewish history with Job and
Abraham. Kierkegaard pays a great deal of attention in his

---

*It appears that the expression "nothing" in Kierkegaard covers the whole
religious sphere of paganism from the most primitive forms to the more refined
ones. All of these forms appear in the light of Christianity as "nothing," produced
by man himself. Kierkegaard can find support for this in Paul's analogy in 1
Corinthians 8:4, which is quoted by Kierkegaard in *S.V.* VI, p. 348; *Stages on
Life's Way,* p. 341.

writing to these two ground-breaking events. In *Repetition* and in *Fear and Trembling* he introduces the ethical and gives his own personal experiences of the ethical in the guise of the old stories of Job and Abraham. In *Philosophical Fragments* and in *Concluding Unscientific Postscript* he describes the ethical stand-point of Socrates.

Socrates discovers the eternal truth within himself, and with this discovery the aesthetic, which until now has monopolized paganism, is set aside. Socrates' irony has penetrated this world's weakness, and from now on nothing in this world can have an absolute value for him. Even the actuality of the state and the community, which in the pagan world occupied first place, had to recede into the background. For Socrates the idea of the Absolute Good—with its demand upon him—comes to rank higher than the laws of the state and the community's accepted standards of morality. After irony has reduced the aesthetic to something of indifferent value, Socrates introduces a new attitude toward, and a new evaluation of, the aesthetic, i.e., the temporal within paganism. In his inner self Socrates possesses more than the world can give him. The inner self, being the Eternal, is greater than all aesthetic externalities.

For the Jewish people the temporal world is subject to God's lordship and thereby loses its absolute importance. Job experiences that there is something different from, and superior to, the world's justice and that God is Lord of all. He takes and he gives again, and nobody has authority over him. Abraham teaches that obedience to God is of supreme importance and that God has a claim to all temporal existence because he is sovereign Lord. God can demand that man resign the whole temporal world, and his demand is higher than all temporal laws and established moral practices. He can demand the sacrifice of Isaac, and he can give Isaac back again. Sacrifice or resignation, analogous to irony, means that there is something higher than all temporal existence. Because of this something higher, temporal existence changes position for Abraham. For the Jew the significance of the aesthetic and temporal becomes this—that this is the realm where God's will is to be actualized.

We must not, however, overlook the difference between Socrates and Abraham. Socrates has pondered the truth and found it in his inner self; he has attained the truth by "recollection." Abraham, on the other hand, is addressed by the God who is beyond the borders of human understanding and who, seen from this point of view, is the Absurd. Abraham, therefore, is ethically farther along the way to the religious life than Socrates can ever come by his own understanding and ethical orientation.

Not until Christianity appears is a sharp distinction between the temporal and the Eternal possible. In Christ, the Eternal appears concretely and at a particular point in history. From this fact a radically new light is shed on all the relationships of existence. Temporal existence, and along with it aesthetic existence, completely changes character. Christianity, as the "principle"[14] of the spirit, stands in absolute contrast to the aesthetic. The aesthetic must now either subordinate itself completely to the claim of spirit or consolidate itself as a kingdom for itself and rebel against spirit.

Kierkegaard deals with this last and new form of the aesthetic existence in *Either-Or,* which was the first major book in which he addressed the public, and again in *Stages on Life's Way.*

The aesthetic in these two works is not the aestheticism we see in paganism. An aura of innocence still plays over the aestheticism of the pagan man; the absolute Either-Or has not yet been pronounced. After Christianity has come into the world, it demands the absolute subordination of temporal existence to the claim of God. Christ points to an eternal existence, and his will is that man shall grow away from domination by the temporal (the aesthetic) and through his power grow into the new order of things. Now, to remain exclusively within the aesthetic and to take one's position there after Christianity has enlightened one about the truth will only lead one into despair.

Since this world is extremely diverse, there are many and various ways to take up a position in temporality and to be in flight from the Eternal. Therefore, in *Either-Or* and in *Stages on Life's Way* we find descriptions of the various forms of aestheticism, which falls within the category of despair.

We turn first to *Either-Or*. The work begins with the "Diapsalmata," a collection of short lyrical utterances which articulate the position of the man of irony. This man of irony does not believe in the Eternal and therefore loses his foothold in existence. His feelings swing between weeping and laughter, and it is irony which bridges the two. Here are some examples from "Diapsalmata":[15]

Of all the ludicrous things in life, I consider this to be the most ludicrous: busyness—to be a man who hurries through his meals and hurries to his work. When, therefore, I see a fly settle on the nose of such a busy man at a critical moment—or see him splashed by a cart which, in still greater hurry, passes him on the road, or the drawbridge is drawn, or a tile falls down from a roof and kills him—then I laugh heartily. And who could keep from laughing? What do they achieve— these bustling activists? They are like that woman who, in her confusion when the house was burning, rescued the fire tongs. What more do they rescue from life's great conflagration?

Life has become a bitter beverage to me, and yet it must be taken drop by drop—slowly—counting.

The best proof for the misery of existence is that which comes from reflecting upon its glory.

It happened once in a theater that some stage scenery caught fire. The clown appeared before the curtain to inform the public. They thought it a joke and applauded. He repeated his announcement. They applauded still more. I imagine that the end of the world will occur while the wags and wits, who think it all a joke, are applauding.

The longest passage in "Diapsalmata" is an ironic treatment of Hegel's philosophy with its tendency to destroy the ethical. It is significant that the passage begins with a quotation attributed to Socrates, in which he ironically declares that without ethical earnestness everything one does—good or bad—is of equal value. "Marry, and you will repent of it. Do not marry, and you will repent of that also . . ." etc.

From these selections of the "Diapsalmata" alone, it is evident that the man of irony revels in the tragic and comic situations of life. From the ironic point of view nothing of value exists any more in life. The ironic man sees through the nothingness of this world, but he relates himself to the spiritual reality despairingly.

"Diapsalmata" expresses, as a whole, the mood of despairing gladness and glad despair which followed the German romanticists and Hegel after they had construed the Eternal as finite and thereby prepared for the leveling of values.

The book *Either-Or* ends with a little meditation entitled "Ultimatum." The theme is: "The upbuilding truth in the thought that in relationship to God we are always in the wrong." "Ultimatum," with its edifying contents, already points in the direction of the religious. Between the lyrically despairing cries of "Diapsalmata" and "Ultimatum's" running start into the religious, we find sketches of the aesthetic and the ethical stages.

The aesthetic stage is characterized also in the essay: "The Immediate Erotic Stages or the Musical-Erotic," with many and excellent interpretations of the character of Don Juan and a special study of Mozart's musical treatment of the Don Juan theme.

It is characteristic of Kierkegaard to have a predilection for choosing man's relationship to the sexual and erotic to illustrate the aesthetic and the ethical relationships. This is because he knows that the sexual and the erotic are the areas within the aesthetic where man's bondage to temporal existence comes most strongly to the fore. Kierkegaard defines the sexual as "the outpost of one extreme of the synthesis"[16]—or, more explicitly, "the extreme point of the synthesis"[17] and "the extreme of the sensuous."[18]

In other words, if one wishes to describe the lowest level of the aesthetic stage, he must begin with a radical example of sensuousness. Kierkegaard found this example in the story of Don Juan, which he revises for his purpose. Don Juan is a genius at "the extreme tip" of sensuousness. Kierkegaard emphasizes that the phenomenon of a Don Juan was possible only after the arrival of Christianity. "The way in which sensuousness is interpreted in *Don Juan*—as a principle—had never before in the world been interpreted."[19] Don Juan is the protest of sensuousness to Christianity's demand to subordinate sensuality to the spirit. Kierkegaard also declares in this essay that the character of Don Juan as a demonic power is best depicted by music, since the demonic is the essential sphere of music.[20] He praises Mozart for having given Don Juan the perfect musical expression.

Exhibiting a remarkable understanding of the aesthetic in placing Don Juan in the context of the stages, Kierkegaard goes on to scrutinize carefully the concept of tragedy in the essay "The Reflection of Ancient Tragedy in Modern Tragedy." He shows how in the development of tragedy the individual becomes more and more self-conscious and that blind, tragic fate is ultimately explained as the individual's guilt. To illustrate the difference between the ancient and modern concept of tragedy, he uses Antigone, who is viewed first from the Greek and then from the modern point of view.

Through these reflections we are prepared for the essay "Shadowgraphs," where we meet the tragic female characters of modern drama—Marie Beaumarchais, Donna Elvira, and Margrethe. These women, compared to Don Juan, are the reverse of the coin: "To seduce all girls is the masculine expression of the feminine yearning to let herself be seduced once and with all her heart and soul."[21] These women had permitted themselves to be seduced and now ponder wearily whether or not their seducers might still be hiding true love.

Now comes the section called "The Unhappiest Man." To understand it, we must remember that the life of the aesthete swings between two extremes—fortune and misfortune, both under the sign of despair. In Don Juan we have a despairingly fortunate man in the aesthetic sphere—and in "The Unhappiest Man" we meet his opposite. The aesthete cannot come any higher than to swing in anxiety and despair between unbounded fortune and unbounded misfortune. In this section misfortune is commended as a privilege, and the unhappiest man is called, among other things, "the unhappy lover of recollection" (one is reminded of Kierkegaard's own unhappy love) and is given the seat of honor. When, finally, we read the paradoxical statement, "Who is the happiest but the most unfortunate, and who is the unhappiest but the most fortunate?"[22] we detect that discernment of the emptiness of aestheticism is about to break through in the fact that aestheticism is now stabilized in the negative only—in unhappiness. The "unhappiest man" has still not found a way out of his misfortune.

The next section of the book is a review of sorts of "First Love," a comedy in one act by Scribe, translated by J. L. Heiberg. The review is a satire on modern coquetry. The characters assure one another that this is their very first love, but their words are hollow. The review says of the heroine of the play: "Her old falling in love with Charles is frivolous, her new falling in love with Renville is also frivolous. Her whims are frivolous, her anger is frivolous, her defiance is frivolous, her good intentions are also frivolous."[23] But no one wishes to dispense with the outward show of affirming that this is the very first love, and even "when a widower and a widow agree to join their fortunes, each of them bringing five children, they will still on their wedding day assure one another that this love is their first love."[24]

"The Rotation Method: The Theory of Social Prudence" treats very humorously that caricature of human life who makes his appearance when one no longer believes in anything permanent and therefore ventures nothing for his convictions. One gets along in life by shrewd calculations. Prudence teaches one never to tie oneself seriously to anyone; doing so may bring difficulties and hinder the sensuous enjoyment of life. Therefore, as it is humorously put, "Watch out for friendship!"[25] If it is durable, it brings trouble. Again, "Never go in for marriage. Married people promise to love each other for eternity. This is easy enough to do, but it doesn't mean much, for when one is through with the temporal he will certainly be through with the Eternal as well. If, instead of promising eternal love, the parties concerned might say—until Easter, or, until the first of May—this would make sense, for in this case both would actually say something and something which they might possibly stick to."[26] The result of this vacillation is emptiness and boredom, both of which are ironically recommended in this selection.

The first part of *Either-Or,* which deals most extensively with the aesthetic stage, ends with "The Diary of the Seducer." This diary takes up a considerable portion of the first part of the book. The theme of seduction here is of a more desperate character than it was in Don Juan. Don Juan represents the as yet natural impulse; he is spontaneous and unreflective. One could almost say that he is naked masculinity. In Johannes, the principal character of "The Diary of the Seducer," sensuality is brought to another plane. One might say that Johannes has the nature of Faust, who takes Mephistopheles into his service to carry out the seduction. It is the method of the seduction and not the number of the seduced which is important to him. Johannes the Seducer's technique is the culmination of the art of seduction. The vindicating aspects of Don Juan are not found here, for Johannes carries out his plan deliberately and with calculating coolness. "The Diary of the Seducer" can be mistaken for a spicy story—and Kierkegaard was well aware of this danger—but the theme of the book is very serious. Kierkegaard is of the opinion that this book, in addition to describing a specific level of the aesthetic stage, contains valuable observations concerning human life. If one understands how to use it, it may, as Kierkegaard says in one of the *Journals,* "serve as a preliminary work for the most serious research and not just something superficial."[27]

With the help of real-life prototypes, the first part of *Either-Or* gives us a glimpse into the aesthetic stage without, however, defining its exact boundaries. This does not come until the second part of the book, which in substance introduces the ethical stage. Here Judge William, representative of the ethical stage, defines the boundaries for the whole realm of the aesthetic. He is able to do this because he himself has passed through the aesthetic and now, as an ethical man, can—from his new position—survey the whole aesthetic stage. His description of the aesthetic stage fully substantiates the supposition that the aesthetic and the temporal existence go together.

Lucidly and logically Judge William sets up a very completely graded scale of all the possible levels of aesthetic stances. There are a multitude of areas in temporal existence which a man may choose as most important and to which he can relate, and this fact provides a multitude of aesthetic viewpoints.

For example, health, riches, or honor may be considered the greatest values in life, and one may build his whole life on these premises. Again, the development of man's faculties and talents may be regarded to be of primary importance. Named are such talents as "a practical talent, a commercial, mathematical, poetical, artistic, and philosophic talent. Satisfaction or enjoyment in life is sought in the unfolding of this talent."[28]

Thus it is that one gets a try at the aesthete's motto of life: "Enjoy life, or, in other words, live according to your desires."[29] "Now," says the Judge, "it happens very rarely, God be praised, that a man is so unfortunately situated in life that there is a possibility of living only for his desires." If this life-stance achieves the external conditions for its unfolding, it ends by making a monster of man. As historical examples of this position, Kierkegaard cites the Roman emperors Nero and Caligula, who lived by the aesthete's rule of life with appalling consistency. Precisely because they had all the opportunities to live wholly according to their desires they felt the emptiness of life most strongly and were forced to find new desires and new means to hinder the awakening of the idea of the Eternal.

The consequence of this uninhibited vitalistic expression, which does not leave room for the spiritual, is melancholy, "the hysteria of the spirit."[30] The Judge points out that his own age, in which sensuous enjoyment has once more set itself up as a principle, contains the same germs of melancholy and crime as the age of these Roman emperors.

On the next point on the scale of aesthetic life-stances lies a concept of life which teaches, "Enjoy life," this time meaning, "Enjoy *yourself.* In enjoyment you shall enjoy *yourself!*" A "higher reflection" is demanded to live at this level, which is more closely defined as "epicurism."[31] Farther along there is the aesthetic position in which one enjoys his strenuously sought-after independence from external things, a sort of stoical contentment with being able to become independent of all external influences.

All these aesthetic positions have this in common—man has made enjoyment, which in one way or another is conditioned by this temporal world, his highest aim in life. Seen from the ethical side, every one of these attitudes—since the Eternal is absent—is despair.

At the top of the aesthetic scale is the one who has seen through the emptiness and despair of pure aestheticism but will not let it go and intoxicates himself with his own despair. Various hints in the text lead us to believe that this last grade of aestheticism typifies much of Kierkegaard's own situation in that period of his life when he regarded himself as "the most unhappy man"—before he took the decisive step toward the religious stage.

The aesthetic stage is heard of again in the first part of *Stages on Life's Way,* in the section entitled "In Vino Veritas." While in the aesthetic positions in *Either-Or* there is still a lingering possibility of tearing oneself loose from despair and choosing the Eternal, the aesthete in "In Vino Veritas" has cemented himself into solid positions. We are presented with a series of consistently drawn aesthetic stances, all of which represent man's view of woman when he has rejected the Eternal. Here again we have an example of how Kierkegaard uses erotic love to describe the stages.

The aesthetic points of view in "In Vino Veritas" are presented during a banquet, where each of the participants states his views of women and of marriage in a speech. The guests at the banquet are the Young Man, Constantin Constantius, Victor Eremita, the Ladies' Tailor, and Johannes the Seducer. The order of the characters indicates also the progressive scale in the devaluing of women. Kierkegaard has previously used three of these names as pseudonyms: Constantin Constantius as author of *Repetition,* Victor Eremita as the editor of *Either-Or,* and Johannes the Seducer as the author of "The Diary of the Seducer."

The Young Man is the first speaker. He is, as mentioned elsewhere, a man "who still hopes."[32] He sees the relationship between man and woman from its comic side and illustrates his opinions profusely. He considers it a delusion for man and woman to believe that in the consummation of their union they are pursuing their own goal, "for in that very moment the race triumphs over the individual. The race wins while the individuals are reduced to serving it."[33] Of the father's position he says, among other things, "Is paternity an idealized state, or is it the most dreadful of all realities? Is it the greatest good, or is it the extreme enjoyment of one's desires? Is it something that merely happens, or is it the loftiest task?"[34] In this manner the young man discovers contradictions everywhere in the erotic life, contradictions which prevent him from coming into a positive relationship to women.

Constantin Constantius, the next speaker, finds that women can never be taken seriously and must be regarded "solely in the category of a jest."[35] "Woman," he says, "has a prescribed right to be transformed in less than twenty-four hours into the most innocent and forgivable galimatias. Far be it from her honest soul to want to deceive anyone! She meant everything she said. Now she says the opposite, but with the same lovable candor, for she is ready to die for the contrary."[36] Constantin Constantius wants to avoid becoming a fool by taking women seriously.

Victor Eremita sees woman's significance to be in the idealism which she awakens in man, but this happens only if man does not get her in the end. If man wins her, she will drag him down to a lower level. Victor Eremita may therefore say,

It is quite true that through woman ideality comes into life. What would man be without her! Many a man became a genius because of a girl. Many a man became a hero because of a girl. Many a man became a poet because of a girl. Many a man became a saint because of a girl. But he did not become a genius because of the girl he got, for through her he became only a cabinet secretary. He did not become a hero because of the girl he got, for through her he became only a general. He did not become a poet because of the girl he got, for through her he became only a father. He did not become a saint because of the girl he got, for he did not get any, and he wanted only the one he did not get— just as each of the others became a genius, a hero, a poet through the girl he didn't get.[37]

Victor Eremita, too, can find no meaning in marriage and therefore will abstain from it.

The Ladies' Tailor vehemently swears that everything in woman revolves about fashion. He has discovered her weakness in his fashion salon, and now he rants against her, declaring that "fashion is the only thing she ever thinks about and the only thing she thinks about in connection with anything."[38] The Tailor's secret motivation is to bring woman to the point where she will be ridiculous enough to "wear a ring in her nose."[39]

The last of the speakers, Johannes the Seducer, regards woman solely from the point of view of desire. He declares that woman is created to snare man in "all the complexities of finitude."[40] For this purpose she is made so alluring that "no enticement equal to woman has been discovered in the world. There is no enticement so absolute as the enticement of innocence, no temptation so fascinating as the temptation of modesty, and no deception so incomparable as woman."[41] Most men let themselves be enticed and bound by her and become married men, but there are also some like Johannes the Seducer, the so-called "erotics." They want to have their pleasure but do not permit themselves to be tied by woman. "They always nibble at the bait," he says, "but they are never caught."[42] In "The Diary of the Seducer" we are given an illustration of how Johannes the Seducer practices his theory of life. He has devised a perfect system in the art of seduction. In *Concluding Unscientific Postscript* he is called a "marked" and an "extinct individual."[43]

All the aesthetes in "In Vino Veritas" represent man's conception of woman when he has abandoned the Eternal and sees woman only with the eyes of temporal existence.

"In Vino Veritas" reminds one of Plato's "Symposium," in which the participants also discuss love. The essential difference, however, is that in Plato the movement is in the direction of spirit, whereas in "In Vino Veritas" the direction is progressively away from spirit into spiritual desolation.

The condition of the pure aesthete is one of anxiety and despair. Deliverance will come by making room for the principal component of the synthesis—the Eternal.

Man may, however, wish to remain in the aesthetic stage. He may become so immersed in temporality that he refuses to come in touch with the Eternal and to let himself be governed and healed by the Eternal. In this case the aesthete passes over into the demonic existence.

In the demonic, man suffers from "anxiety about the Good"[44] —the Eternal. Man is anxious lest the Eternal should remind him that he is living a lie. The demonic man is obsessed by something temporal, barricades himself in it, and isolates himself from relationship to the Good. In this form the demonic is the extreme manifestation of the aesthetic stage.

Every man begins his life in the aesthetic stage and with the possibility of the Eternal, but if man, anxious about the Good, tries to bar every contact with the Eternal, he will be dominated by the demonic. In *The Concept of Anxiety (Dread)* we have an extensive and thorough treatment of the whole area of the demonic. For the demonic man as well as for the aesthete it holds true that there are many areas in temporality where he may take root—from a completely animalistic absorption in the temporal to more conscious forms. But in all of them man is dominated by anxiety about the Good. The chapter on the demonic in *The Concept of Anxiety* concludes with a clear definition of the essentially demonic: "But men are not willing to think earnestly about the Eternal. They are anxious about it, and anxiety discovers a hundred ways of escape. But this, precisely, is what it is to be demonic."[45]

With his definition of the demonic as the outpost of the aesthetic stage Kierkegaard reaches the deepest and darkest corners of the human soul. Kierkegaard's characterization reveals how the human soul can bind itself completely to something temporal, how it encompasses this thing and—creating its own anguish and ruin—tries to rid itself of the thought of the Eternal. Deeper than the uncovering of this whole domain of the secret depths of the human soul no psychology can reach.

# III. *The Ethical Stage*

To Kierkegaard the ethical stage means, first of all, that the Eternal with its claims has impinged upon a man, and second, that he believes in the possibility of fulfilling these claims in the temporal world. Whereas in the aesthetic stage the whole center of gravity lies in the temporal world and the individual has not and does not will to have an eternal self, an eternal I, in the ethical stage man with a consciousness of his eternal significance is in the center. The ethical stage points farther, to the third and last center of gravity, to the thought of God and his reality. On the ethical level one learns how much or how little he can do by himself and where the essential goals of human life are to be found.

It is possible to distinguish between the various gradations of development also in the ethical stage. At the lowest level of the ethical stage one still believes that he is able to fulfill the claims of the Eternal and that it is possible to do so within the boundaries of temporality. The ethical stage culminates in the understanding of how tenaciously a man is bound to temporality and how little he achieves by his own endeavors. In this last awareness the center moves from man to God.

As mentioned before, at two points in world history a transition was effected from the morality which still lies within the compass of aestheticism (temporality) to the ethical, which always has its ground in faith in the Eternal beyond the boundaries of the visible. The transition came to the Hebrew people through Job and Abraham and in paganism through Socrates.

Job fights the "frontier battle"[46] between the human and the divine interpretation of justice and is matured for faith in a new and higher order of things than that which a man can grasp with his own reasoning and calculating. The transition to the ethical is illustrated still more clearly in the story of Abraham. After God has called Abraham, his life comes under divine authority. He becomes responsible to a Lord who stands infinitely higher than all the moral laws and customs of this world. The claims which this Power can make upon Abraham are higher than his responsibilities to the family and the community. The community—or the universal—has temporal goals. Here the individual stands lower than the universal and must surrender himself completely to the laws of the community. By coming into relationship with an eternal Power, the individual acknowledges higher obligations than those of the community and visible authorities. Therefore Kierkegaard states in *Fear and Trembling* that Abraham relates himself to the paradox[47]—that is, to a Power which exceeds the boundaries of the visible and so also the boundaries of human understanding. When the individual steps into relationship with this Power, he becomes isolated from the community and cannot make himself understood by it. The claims of the universal must always be confirmed and be explained by the interests of the community, but God is not accountable either to the individual or to the universal, and God can issue commands which are contrary to the universally human law. God can bring a person into conflict with these laws and can demand their suspension.

Abraham moves from a purely moral position through the ethical and crosses the frontier into the religious. Abraham's sacrifice of Isaac expresses the ethical-religious position in which man, out of obedience to God, is willing to suspend the moral laws and to isolate himself from the community. By this act Abraham, in humble faith, surrenders his own reasonable calculation and enters into the paradox.

The sacrifice of Isaac as an ethical-religious act is demanded of Abraham only this once. Essentially he lives his everyday life within ethical categories. He has faith in the Eternal, and he submits his temporal existence to the eternal claims of the laws of God.

Abraham's sacrifice marks the beginning of an ethical revolution in a people, and Judaism strove zealously to establish God's commands in the temporal world. This ethical position is borne up by an initial optimism which characterizes the beginning of the ethical stage. Abraham is "the righteous man,"[48] and he can—in obedience—fulfill God's claims upon him. A long historical experience is necessary before man in Judaism begins to doubt his ability to fulfill the laws of God. This scepticism does not break through clearly until Judaism is confronted with Christianity. By this time Judaism has tried its strength. The law has ceased to be an attainable ideal for the Jews and has become an accuser and a discipliner. About this last station on the way Kierkegaard says:

There was already a deep irony in relation to the world when the law, having proclaimed the commandments, added the promise: if you fulfill these, you will be blessed—since it became apparent that precisely what men cannot do is to fulfill the law—and therefore a blessedness, connected with this condition, became more than hypothetical. The self-annihilation of Judaism appears precisely in its historic relation to Christianity.[49]

Within paganism the possibility of an ethical outlook came first with Socrates. Socrates had come to the conviction that we can never attain an absolute truth by exploring the visible (temporal) world. By using this method we find only relative truths or truths which hold true only for this transient world. In man's inwardness there is the possibility of a higher knowledge than is to be found by exploring the outer world. Every man possesses in his inner self the possibility of a knowledge of eternal truths; by plumbing the depths of his own being— by "recollection"—man can discover these truths.

As a consequence of this Socratic understanding, the laws of the state and the universe are no longer the highest, since man in his inwardness possesses knowledge of a reality higher than the state. Moreover, the individual, in this pagan view, is higher than the social-historical universal. Therefore Socrates views with irony man's bustling activities inside the boundaries of a purely temporal existence, where no absolute contradictions are to be found, and he regards what a man chooses in life to be a matter of indifference if he does not come to know the Eternal. One is reminded of his ironical answer to one of these busy men, which goes something like this: "Marry or do not marry. You will repent of both!"

Life becomes earnest for the first time with knowledge of the Eternal. The individual then has the task of uniting the Eternal and the temporal in his existence. By this conception man is placed in the center of existence, as is stated in *Philosophical Fragments:* "In the Socratic view every man is himself the center of existence, and the whole world focuses upon him because his self-knowledge is a God-knowledge."[50] Socrates considers it his task to call men's attention to his discovery.

This Socratic insight forms the point of departure for man's ethical activity. Socrates' understanding and actualization of the ethical standpoint are formulated in *Concluding Unscientific Postscript* in the sentence: "Subjectivity is truth." Since this quotation from Kierkegaard is very familiar and very often misunderstood, we shall try to explain it precisely. That "subjectivity is truth" means simply that a man tries to act in accordance with the eternal truth which he finds in his innermost being. In this way the Eternal, which was only an abstract knowledge, acquires a personal meaning for a man. We may therefore state this sentence another way: the Eternal is truth —or, even better, inwardness is truth. From this it is clear that the statement "Subjectivity is truth" disassociates itself from the interpretation that truth is subjective and arbitrary so that every man may decide for himself what is the truth. This, precisely, is the significance of Socrates—that he points away from the arbitrary understanding of truth which was practiced in his age especially by the Sophists. Truth, which Socrates found in his inwardness, is an eternal and universal truth, and it can become a personal and living truth in each individual who wills to avail himself of it in his life. This, then, is the meaning of the "Socratic wisdom,"[51] as it is called in *Concluding Unscientific Postscript.*

Socrates still has the untried ethical man's confidence that man can easily fulfill the ethical claims in his life. He believes that the chief difficulty lies on the side of self-knowledge. If a man comprehends the truth, he will act accordingly. Kierkegaard, who values Socrates highly, has to admit that at this point Socrates' insight was insufficient. Socrates, and along with him the "Greek intellect, was too happy, too naive, too aesthetic, too ironic, too witty, too sinful to get it through his head that someone with knowledge might fail to do the good, or with knowledge—with knowledge of what is right—would do the wrong."[52] The way was still long from Socrates to the new insight that man in his subterranean depths clings tenaciously to untruth.

Before we leave Socrates and go on to the next levels of the ethical stage, mention should be made that in *Philosophical Fragments,* that strictly logically constructed book of Kierkegaard's, Socrates, as a representative of the highest human wisdom, is compared to Christ. Kierkegaard's purpose is to show clearly the difference between the best of human nature and "the God." We shall treat these characterizations under the religious stage.

In *Either-Or* and *Stages on Life's Way,* through the person of Judge William, Kierkegaard informs us of the next levels of the ethical stage. Judge William's two discourses on the ethical life, besides serving as descriptions of the next levels of the ethical stage, demonstrate how this stage of human existence is developed and re-formed within the same person.

In *Either-Or* Judge William represents an early position in the development of the ethical being. This is noticeable throughout his whole discourse. He is inspired by the Socratic confidence that if only one knows the truth one can easily make it valid in his life. In letters to the Young Man, the aesthete who is supposed to have written the first part of *Either-Or,* he describes the new life of the ethical stage and tells how one can and must make the leap from the aesthetic to the ethical.

The Judge is very familiar with Christianity. As an ethical man he understands the claim of Christianity to be that a man must allow the Eternal to pervade all his relationships in life. He also understands that a man is strongly bound to the temporal and that the beginning of finding oneself can only be made, as he says, by repenting oneself out of rootage in the temporal.[53] The principal factor in his position is precisely this —that he has discovered his eternal self and has chosen him-

self. The Judge therefore believes that "the moment one becomes conscious of one's eternal worth is more meaningful than
everything else in the world."[54] In a moving way he describes
*this* moment, *the* moment when the transition from the aesthetic
to the ethical stage is accomplished:

> When all has become silent around one, solemn as a starlit night,
> when the soul becomes alone in the whole world—then before one
> appears—not a remarkable man—but the eternal Power himself. Then
> heaven will seem to open, and the I chooses itself, or, more correctly,
> receives itself. Then the soul has seen the ultimate—that which no mor-
> tal eye can see—and which never can be forgotten. Then the individual
> receives the salutation which elevates him forever.[55]

Not until this choice has been made will there be an absolute
distinction between good and evil, between an absolute either-
or. In the aesthetic stage these differences are only relative.

With the inward transformation which the consciousness of
his personal worth gives him, the ethical person proceeds to the
solution of the concrete tasks. Back in the temporal again, he
seeks to make a synthesis of the temporal and the eternal. The
Judge elaborates on his new understanding of the tasks in life,
vigorously attacks aestheticism, and warns against the dangers
in it which threaten the ethical man. He labors earnestly to
prove the possibility of creating a synthesis between the aesthetic and the ethical, that is, between the temporal and the
Eternal. The Judge warns his young friend, the aesthete, that
living only within "the aesthetic view of life is despair."[56] He
desires to awaken the aesthete "to despair" over the finite in
order that he may venture the transition to the ethical stage.

Already, in the realm of the aesthetic, the Judge finds a pre-
sentiment of something eternal. In erotic love—in romantic
love—the lovers experience a feeling of belonging together
eternally. The Judge wishes to rescue this ideal from aestheticism
and let it become an important factor in the ethical understand-

ing of the relationship between man and woman. From an ethical point of view, only a marriage contracted before God is the right expression for the relationship between man and woman. He draws attention to the fact that marriage, ideally speaking, "belongs essentially to Christianity" and that "in spite of the sensuousness of the East and all the beauty of Greece the pagans did not perfect it," and "not even Judaism with all its truly idyllic elements was able to achieve it." The Judge maintains further that "in Christianity, too, love has to pass through many experiences before one comes to see the depths, the beauty, and the truth which lie in marriage."[57]

The Judge discourses at length on marriage, for, according to his viewpoint, marriage is the center of existence. He tries to speak of marriage as it ought to be according to his conception. Such a marriage should contain two factors: love and a relationship to God. Through the relationship to God the lovers receive their love as a gift from God and as a task from God's hand.

Since love, and even more so marriage, contains an eternal factor, there can be no exhaustive justification for them. A justification for marriage based only on temporal and finite considerations is inadequate. Quite humorously the Judge demolishes the three principal arguments for marriage: to marry "in order to cultivate one's character," or "to get children," or "to get a home."[58] Having set these three motives aside, he says: "I have mentioned these three only because they always seem to make sense, because they reflect in one way or another particular factors in marriage, even though in their one-sidedness they become just as ludicrous as they are unaesthetic and irreligious. I will not mention a host of contemptible, finite reasons because one cannot even laugh at them!"[59]

The Judge goes on to say that the primary condition on which marriage should be grounded is "openness, sincerity, and pub-

lic declaration according to the loftiest standard, for this is the
vital principle of love, and secretiveness here means its death."[60]
He explains further how this condition is to be practiced in life.
The Judge also tries to justify to the young aesthete the solemn
wedding ceremony when entering into marriage.

After the Judge has attempted to grapple with the dangers
which threaten from aestheticism, and after he has shown how
the aesthetic can be subordinated to the ethical, he turns to
another danger. He comes to grips with the mystic's position.
In the case of the aesthete the danger is that he will not have
anything to do with the Eternal. The opposite is true for the
mystic. The mystic has chosen the Eternal, but he clings only to
that, and the temporal completely loses its meaning for him.
"The mystic," declares the Judge, "chooses himself abstractly.
One may therefore say that he continuously chooses himself out
of the world, but as a consequence he cannot choose himself back
into the world again."[61] Because of his ethical position and his
special emphasis on the meaning of marriage, the Judge has to
reject completely the mystic's position. His attack on the mystic
implies a clear repudiation of the medieval monastic movement.

Toward the end of his discourse the Judge reviews such
practical subjects as a man's relationship to his work and to
his concern for getting his daily bread. Speaking of man's work,
the Judge contradicts the aesthete's talk about talents and says
that every human being should consider his work as a calling.

In *Either-Or* the Judge is quite sure of himself and presents
his human-ethical views with the quiet force of conviction. In
*Stages on Life's Way* he is a little older and more experienced
and has discovered more difficulties than he imagined at the
beginning. His whole presentation is now sustained by a more
humorous touch. His attacks on aestheticism are more vigorous,
and at the same time he speaks of marriage so warmly that one

almost believes he is about to repudiate his views on marriage and for that reason wishes to say so many good things about it! He has discovered how instructive a marriage can be, and in his introduction to the work he issues a humorous invitation to the state of matrimony:

> My dear Reader! In case you do not have either the time or the opportunity to spend ten years of your life traveling around the world to see everything the globe-trotter sees, in case you have neither the talent for foreign languages nor the occasion of many years of usage so that you become familiar with the distinctive and individual national differences which are revealed to students of languages; in case you do not harbor the intention of discovering a new astronomical system which will supplant both the Copernican and the Ptolemaic systems—then go and get married. In the event that you have time for the first, talent for the second, and an inclination to do the last—then go and get married *just the same!* Even if you don't get around to seeing the whole terrestrial planet or speaking in many languages or comprehending the heavens, you will not regret it, for marriage is and remains the most important journey of discovery a man can undertake. Every other kind of acquaintance with existence is superficial compared to that acquired by a married man—for he and he alone has thoroughly fathomed the depths of human existence.[62]

The Judge is well acquainted with all the attacks on woman and marriage which the aesthetes expound in "In Vino Veritas" and rejects them energetically. It is noteworthy, however, that the Judge now admits that the way to the ideal is difficult, but he consoles himself with the fact that "one can still be a happy husband without having attained perfection if one only keeps the ideal in view and humbly feels his imperfection."[63] The Judge is aware, also, that he has "pegged the price up a bit" and has set the ideal so high that it is difficult to practice it.

The problem of the relationship between erotic love as the highest pagan love and marriage is gone into more profoundly, and marriage emerges as "a higher expression of love."[64] From the Judge's ethical viewpoint, marriage is still to be regarded as "the highest goal of individual human existence,"[65] and he goes so far in his estimation of marriage that he can say: "Marriage is the beautiful midpoint and center of life and of human existence, reflecting the depths and the heights of that which it makes known—a revelation which in a hidden way uncovers heaven."[66]

Coherent with all this is the Judge's spirited eulogy of woman as wife and mother. Nothing more beautiful can be said on this subject than what the Judge says in *Stages on Life's Way*. It seems as if he wants to remove the sting from the aesthete's attack on woman, especially when he stresses the fact that woman does not develop to her fullest until she is regarded from the ethical.

Here are a few examples of the Judge's defense of woman:

> Woman is more beautiful as a bride than as a maiden; as mother she is more beautiful than as a bride. As mother she is a good word spoken at the right time, and she becomes more beautiful with the years.[67]
>
> A woman's life as a mother is a reality so infinitely rich and varied that my ardor has enough to do in discovering what is new each day. A woman as mother has no situation in which she can be said to be most beautiful and at her best; as mother she is always in this situation. Mother love is soft as pure gold, relaxed in every way, yet whole.[68]
>
> How numerous the collisions which mother love encounters, and how beautiful the mother when her self-denying, self-sacrificing love comes through the conflicts victoriously.[69]

The Judge can see more clearly now that the marriage resolution can be maintained and the difficulties in marriage can be overcome only if one believes in God "in all dangers and temptations."[70] The Judge is beginning to comprehend the inadequacy of all human endeavors. He is on the way to a religious crisis in which the center of gravity shifts from man, from the human, to God. As yet marriage is to him "the center in the temporal,"[71] and the married man "feels no lack of the Eternal, for it is with him in the temporal."[72] But the Judge finally makes an admission in the discourse which shatters his former point of view. He expresses it thus: "I do not say that marriage is the most sublime life. I know one more sublime. But woe to him who without justification wants to skip over marriage."[73]

In the last pages of his discourse the Judge investigates what circumstances there might be which would justify a transition from the stage he represents to a higher one. He speaks earnestly and urgently about the "terror"[74] and about the sufferings which wait for the one who becomes involved in the religious life. He advises against giving up too soon the quiet happiness of the human-ethical stage to make unwarranted entry into the religious stage.

# IV. *The Religious Stage*

With the Judge's discourse in *Stages on Life's Way* we reach the border between the ethical and the religious stages. The Judge discovers there the difficulties of fulfilling the ethical. He had vigorously set upon the task of incorporating the Eternal into the temporal and had believed at first that he might succeed. The center of gravity for all his efforts was in the temporal world. Through his attempt, the Judge comes to realize the inadequacy of merely human endeavor. At the same time he comes to see that the goal of human existence lies outside the borders of the visible world. With this insight the center of gravity in man's spiritual development moves from man himself to God.

It must, however, be emphasized that the ethical stage also rests upon a religious premise. In Kierkegaard's understanding, the ethical stage is impossible without an apprehension of God. Thus Abraham's sacrifice of Isaac was a religious act, although Abraham otherwise acted on strictly ethical principles in his daily life, and Socrates' ethical position approached "the border of the religious."[75] Finally, we have seen the Judge as an ethical being finding his way into repentance, which expresses a religious outlook. But in all these positions the religious is only secondary, since all the representatives still believe in the possibility of accomplishing by themselves a temporal-Eternal synthesis and are still free from the skepticism which shows itself for the first time at the end of the ethical stage—a skepticism as to whether man in his depths wills the good and can attain it himself. From the religious standpoint, it appears that even man's best endeavors in the human-ethical domain are basically an expression of self-assertion. "If the individual is inwardly dialectical in self-assertion in such a way that his deepest ground does not become dialectical, since the underlying self is used for conquering and for asserting itself—then we have the *ethical interpretation*."[76] As long as a man believes in his own ability to do the good and refuses to admit how strongly he is attached to the temporal, he is still in the ethical stage. On the last level of the ethical stage man doubts his ability to do the good and, like the Judge in *Stages,* he appraises the results of his own efforts with a sense of humor. Thus humor comes to draw the boundary line between the ethical and the religious.

Through Christianity a man comes to know for the first time how deeply he is grounded in evil, and not until he has this realization is it possible for a "radical cure"[77] to begin. However, the religious stage also has many levels. As shown previously, man comes to the religious position through his unsuccessful attempts to accomplish on his own the ethical demands upon him. It may happen, however, that without having lived through the ethical stage a man begins with a skepticism about his own capacity and willingness to do the good. If a man has experienced his tie to the temporal in a unique way, he may be prevented from anchoring in the human-ethical position after having resolved to cast away from the aesthetic standpoint. It becomes a simple matter of necessity to leap over the ethical

stage and begin the religious. This was the case with Kierkegaard himself.

Through his heritage,* through his rigorous Christian upbringing,** and through the experiences of his youth,***
Kierkegaard gains insights into the spiritual fact "that there
are sins from which a man can be saved only by extraordinary,
divine help."[78] For this reason he was unable, as he says, "to
realize the universal"[79] with the same happy, confident certainty
which the Judge and most other people possess. Kierkegaard
was placed outside of the human ethical position in which marriage forms the center of life. He had to pay dearly for his
attempt in this direction with Regine Olsen. Kierkegaard's road
took him farther into the religious position with which he was
well acquainted, but from the beginning it was never clear to
him how far he should venture out in it and whether there was
a possibility of marriage for him under the new presuppositions.
Kierkegaard came to the conclusion that he had to break his
engagement to Regine because he lacked the chief qualification
for marriage, that which the ethical demands—namely, the
ability to take each other into full confidence. Kierkegaard
could not take Regine into the secrets of his life, and this fact
leads him past the ethical stage into the religious.

---

*"An old man, himself tremendously melancholy (how it came about I will
not write), gets a son in his old age, a son who inherits all this melancholy—
but who also has the spiritual elasticity to conceal it. While his melancholy cannot overpower him because his spirit is essentially and supremely sound, the spirit
fails to dissolve the melancholy but strongly influences him to bear it . . ."
(*Pap.* VII A 126).
**"As a child I was strictly and earnestly brought up in Christianity—humanly
speaking, insanely brought up. Already in earliest childhood I had overstrained
myself bearing the sensibilities beneath which the melancholy old man who had
laid them upon me himself sank. A child—insanely dressed up like a melancholy
old man" (*S.V.* XIII, p. 564. *The Point of View for My Work as an Author*,
p. 76).
***"I was knocked about in life, tempted by a multitude of extremely differ-
ent things—worse yet, by delusions and, alas, by the way of perdition . . ."
(*S.V.* XIII, p. 576; *Ibid.* p. 80).

What these secrets were is an open question, but I agree with those researchers who seek the secrets in the six papers inserted in the third section of *Stages on Life's Way*. Here Kierkegaard describes poetically how through great sufferings he breaks the engagement. It is reasonable for him to give also here some inkling of the direction in which his problems lay. The titles of these interpolations are:[80] "The Quiet Despair," "A Leper's Soliloquy," "Solomon's Dream," "A Possibility," "A School Exercise," and "Nebuchadnezzar." It is impossible in this short introduction to go into an interpretation of these papers. We can only take a look at their essential concern.*

Kierkegaard, who, because of his imagination and his excellent powers of reflection, felt himself superior to his age,[81] had certain aspects in his life of possible physical, psychical, or spiritual origin which brought him anguish and were the reasons for his melancholy. He gradually came to understand that his problems were compensation for his superior faculties. These torments and his melancholy also revealed to him the dark side of existence and taught him at the same time how much man is attached to the temporal world, something he felt especially when it was denied him to live his life in an ordinary way. To be set outside of the universal in this way may tempt a man to revolt against God. Because of his sufferings, Kierkegaard was early placed in the position where he must either end in demonic despair or fight on beyond the human optimistic position to what he calls "the second spontaneity."[82] After having an experience in May of 1838 resembling Paul's ecstasy, Kierkegaard took a higher view of his sufferings and understood that what he later calls "the thorn in the flesh" was the price for

---

*Among the attempts at a coherent treatment of the interpolated pieces, mention should be made of Hans Ellekilde's treatise, *Studier i Søren Kierkegaards Ungdomsliv,* and Lina Zeuthen's very detailed book, *Søren Kierkegaards hemmelige Noter,* works not yet available in English.

his experience of "an indescribable joy."[83] Kierkegaard discovered that suffering and joy belong together. This view is
confirmed in his edifying literature.

With the edifying discourses we arrive at the central part of
Kierkegaard's authorship, in which he characterizes the levels
in the religious development. This sketch of the levels also
gives us the progress of Kierkegaard's own development and
shows us how he struggled to free himself from the demonic
and to come deeper into the ethical-religious stage. It also
helped Kierkegaard to understand more deeply the religious
existence which he desired Regine to know when he edited his
first edifying discourse. It very possibly laid the groundwork
for his own later progress, for Kierkegaard—to repeat—was
from the very beginning not clear about how far he should venture into the religious existence.

Kierkegaard classifies the religious stage into two primary
divisions: Religion A and Religion B. Religion A means that
the individual has realized his own bondage to the temporal
and his own insufficiency and now wills to relate himself to all
things only through God. In Religion A the individual will
consequently become conscious of his own nothingness in relation to God, but he has not entirely relinquished the action of
his own goodness. He still relates himself to Christ only as a
prototype—not as Savior, the relationship which is characteristic
of Religion B.

In Religion A the individual expresses his understanding of
existence by trying to relate himself absolutely to the Eternal
and relatively to the temporal.* He begins by making room for
God's claims. This is what Kierkegaard expressed existentially

---

*For better understanding I have altered the phrase in *S.V.* VII, p. 375, about
"relating oneself absolutely to the absolute and relatively to the relative" goals,
to one with the identical meaning: relating oneself "absolutely to the Eternal
and relatively to the temporal" (*Concluding Unscientific Postscript*, p. 386).

in breaking his engagement with Regine. The subject of his first eighteen discourses is resignation. The individual learns in everything to bend his will to the demands of God and to endure patiently his destiny. Among these discourses is the significant "The Thorn in the Flesh,"* which gives a religious explanation of Kierkegaard's sufferings. The last discourse in this collection teaches the meaning of prayer. "The righteous man strives in prayer with God and conquers in that God conquers."[84] The main point of the discourses is this: away with human self-reliance to risk oneself out upon "the seventy thousand fathoms of water."[85] This daring act is the beginning of the journey on the religious way.

After the eighteen edifying discourses, Kierkegaard published "Three Discourses on Imagined Occasions." The first discourse treats man's aspiration toward God and his meeting with God and gives a deep insight into the development of man's conception of God. The second discourse begins with a wedding and strongly stresses the gravity of the vow and the responsibility to God in establishing a marriage. The last discourse is a solemn, enlightening meditation on death, which brings an end to temporal life. None of these discourses has yet arrived at the distinctively Christian. For this there must first be a long preparation.

One aspect of the Christian position appears in the next collection: *Edifying Discourses in Various Spirits.* The collection consists of three parts. The first describes how the individual tears himself away from the multiplicity of this world through repentance and seeks that purity of heart which consists of "in truth to will the good."[86] The four dangers which confront the

---

*S.V. V, pp. 106-123; *Edifying Discourses,* Vol. IV, pp. 49-73. See also my article, "Paelen i Kødet hos Søren Kierkegaard" in *Dansk teologisk Tidsskrift,* 3, 1940, 82-90.

individual when he earnestly wills the good are comprehensively treated. The first danger is to will the good for the sake of reward. The second is to will the good from fear of punishment. The third is to will the good self-assertively; the fourth, to will the good up to a point. The good must be willed for its own sake. "A person must be willing to do everything for the sake of the good and be willing to suffer everything for the sake of the good."[87] Here in this challenge we begin to see clearly the preparation for Christianity's demands as Kierkegaard understood them.

The second portion of *Edifying Discourses in Various Spirits,* three sermons under the title "What We Can Learn from the Lilies of the Field and the Birds of the Sky," deals very simply with this text from the Gospels. The first sermon instructs us to cast off temporal cares; the second reminds man of his eternal purpose; the third discusses the choice between God and Mammon and the glory of the kingdom of God.

The third portion of *Edifying Discourses in Various Spirits* leads us into the Christian demand for discipleship. This section marks the individual's growth from immediacy into the Eternal. The second element in the synthesis, the Eternal, is stressed more and more strongly. This whole new relationship expresses the law which Kierkegaard has formulated: to relate oneself absolutely to the Eternal and relatively to the temporal. It is hereby decisively affirmed that the goal of human life lies beyond the temporal and that it is man's task to get clear about this relationship and to build his life in such a way that he is not bound to that which he must lose. He who takes this position in earnest must inevitably suffer in this world, and thus suffering becomes the characteristic mark of the religious life. But suffering is not the only mark of the religious stage. One recalls that the lower stages had contrapuntal life qualities.

The aesthete's goal was enjoyment and pleasure, but this recipro-
cated with emptiness and tedium. The ethically orientated man
had a battle which yielded an inner contentment. Similarly, the
suffering in the religious stage has a counterpart. It is joy, a
joy which nothing and nobody can take away.

In order not to discourage the individual by having to emphasize suffering as essential to the religious position, Kierkegaard
is accustomed to speaking of joy together with suffering. One
sees this in the third part of the book, where Kierkegaard introduces most of the seven sermons, which aim to familiarize us
with the Christian demand, with a sentence beginning: "The
joy in the fact that . . ."—for example, "The joy in the fact that
the school of suffering educates for eternity. . . ." In these seven
discourses Kierkegaard stresses a side of Christianity which
generally is neglected in the Lutheran church—discipleship.
Since we cannot deal with each discourse separately, we will
look at the central one, the fourth: "The joy in the fact that man
in his relation to God always suffers as one who is guilty."[88]

This is the third time that Kierkegaard treats the same subject—each time from a higher point of view. The first time is
in the book *Repetition,* where Job asserts his righteousness before God but finally has to recognize his unrighteousness. The
second time is in the last portion of *Either-Or,* "Ultimatum,"
with the discourse "The Edification in the Thought That in Relation to God We Are Always in the Wrong," where man's unrighteousness before God is even more strongly emphasized.
The same theme occurs again in the third part of *Edifying Discourses in Various Spirits,* but from a higher point of view.
Here there is no more talk of wrong, but of guilt, in the relationship to God. In his anguish when he was at the point of
revolting against God, Kierkegaard consoled himself with these
thoughts about a man's wrong and a man's guilt in relation to

God. These reflections may help others in the same situation. There are times and occasions when a man considers himself or others to be suffering innocently in this world. It is also true that in their mutual relationships men can be more guilty or less guilty. But in our relation to God we are always—no matter what happens—unrighteous and guilty. To think otherwise is the same as trying to abolish God or to revolt against him. Kierkegaard points out in the discourse that the only one who suffered innocently in this world was Christ.

The theme which Kierkegaard develops in the next edifying works does not emphasize grace as much as obeying the Christian demands. Therefore Kierkegaard is often accused of neglecting grace. Perhaps this is the proper time to deal with this question and to refute this accusation as unjustified. Kierkegaard perceived very early that a one-sided emphasis on grace—especially in Lutheran countries—had reached a point where this central Christian truth was losing its meaning. He understood very well that the higher the truth, the greater and more dangerous is the misuse to which it is exposed. Such is also the case with this most important concept of Christianity—grace. Grace has meaning only when a man has earnestly searched his own heart and has come to the painful but redeeming discovery of how little he can himself achieve. Grace finds its rightful place only against this background. The right understanding and receiving of grace presuppose a man who always has God's demands hanging over his head, who tries to fulfill them but is convinced again and again of his own inadequacy and accepts grace as a gift. It also means that grace always presupposes the presence of, and responsibility to, a higher ethic than social morality. If we believe that the highest ideal to which we are to conform is merely social morality, then grace loses all its meaning. Fundamentally, we are able to obey ordinary civil laws. There, at least, we do not need to fall short. Not until God comes with his commandments and laws, which are even more sharply defined by Christianity—preparing us for an eternal existence—not until then does man, through the recognition of his weakness, mature to the right use of grace. One may perhaps express it thus: By its demands upon the individual, Christianity creates in him the recognition of his own insufficiency and then comes to his aid with grace. Thus Kierkegaard tries to protect the individual from misusing grace. He says: "I will present the Christian demand—discipleship—in all its infiniteness in order to thrust the individual in the direction of grace."[89] It was very clear to him that "demoralization may follow upon the rigorous preaching of the law, but the most dangerous demoralization is and will always be the demoralization with the help of grace."[90] Kierkegaard's emphasis on the Christian demand is quite understandable when we consider that he wants to prevent grace from being taken in vain.*

Bearing these things in mind, we turn to the book *Works of Love,* which, according to Kierkegaard, is "the fruit of much

---

*" 'And what, then, does this all mean?' It means that everyone by himself, in quiet inwardness before God, is to humble himself under what it means in the most rigorous sense to be a Christian and honestly to confess before God how it is with him, so that he might nevertheless receive worthily the grace which is offered to every imperfect man, that is, to everyone. . . . If anything else is required of him, God will surely let him understand and in that case also help him; for the terrible language of the law is so terrifying because it seems as if man himself should hold fast to Christ by his own power, whereas in the language of love it is Christ who holds him fast. . . . To be a Christian has become as nothing, something for simpletons, something which everyone is automatically, something into which one slides more easily than into the most trivial habit. Truly it is high time that the requirement of ideality be heard.

" 'But if Christianity is something so terrifying and frightening, how in all the world can it occur to a man to accept Christianity?' It is very simple, and if you so desire, very Lutheran: only the consciousness of sin can force, if one may say it this way (from the other side it is the force of grace), one into this frightfulness. And at the same moment Christianity transforms itself into perfect mildness, grace, love, compassion." *S.V.,* XII, pp. 64-65. *Training in Christianity,* p. 71.

reflection."[91] The two parts of this book are permeated with
the highest Christian pathos. In this work Kierkegaard describes
Christian love, which is based upon the commandment: "Thou
shalt love thy neighbor as thyself." He then compares this
Christian love with different forms of human love. The principal theme of the book, then, is love of neighbor, which is
eulogized as the only true love, since it is grounded in the relationship to God. Kierkegaard points out that paganism did
not know love of neighbor as an absolute demand. Judaism,
although it had received the commandment to love the neighbor, generally preferred keeping the negative commandments
which begin with "Thou shalt not." Christianity regards the
positive essence of the commandments—love of neighbor—
as most important and calls for its practical fulfillment.

Love of neighbor always has its origin in God and cannot be
exercised without self-renunciation. Kierkegaard points out that
"what the world honors and loves as love is union in self-
love."[92] Christianity demands that one should love himself and
his neighbor according to the Eternal's idea of love—that is,
not by promoting each other's egotism but by helping each
other to self-renouncing love. From this viewpoint friendship
and erotic love are also self-love, since, if God does not come
between as the middle term, they are founded on preference
and inclination. These human forms of love can be sanctified
by first loving the other person as one's neighbor. In one's
friend, in one's beloved, and in one's wife, one must first and
foremost love one's neighbor, and one must continue to do so
however much the love which rises from inclinations and feelings changes. One must everywhere be on guard so "that no
love and no expression of love may temporally or just humanly
be deprived of the relationship to God."[93]

In *Works of Love* Kierkegaard attempts to show how Christian love expresses itself in the different relationships of life. Special attention is called to his reflections on social differences in this world and on how Christianity alone can be of any help here. Christianity does not attempt to abolish the social differences, for they can never be abolished. On the contrary, by calling for an inner revolution in man by love of neighbor, Christianity attacks self-love, which is the root of all unrighteousness in the world. It is certainly noteworthy that Kierkegaard's challenge in *Works of Love* to solve all problems by self-renunciation appeared only a few months before another challenge to solve social problems by force—the *Communist Manifesto* of Karl Marx, which was published in February, 1848. Kierkegaard and Marx toss out to the world their totally opposite views on the solution of life's problems. In *Works of Love* Kierkegaard indicts all outward progress which has forgotten the most important truth. This is quite apparent in statements like this:

*"But the main thing is still this, that need be met in every way, and that everything possible be done to remedy every need."* This is the way the secular world speaks, well-meaning, and it cannot very well speak otherwise. But the Eternal says: There is only one danger—this, that mercifulness is not practiced; even if aid were given in every need, there is still no certainty that it was done in mercifulness, and if this was not the case, this wretchedness—that mercifulness was not practiced at all— would be greater than all temporal need.[94]

Again, " 'Get us money—get us hospitals—these are the most important.' 'No,' says the Eternal, 'the most important is mercifulness.' " Kierkegaard believes that if men succeeded in abolishing all material need in the world—but at the cost of man's withdrawal from God and forgetting the Eternal—this would be a greater misery than all other human misery.

*Works of Love,* with its clear statement of the demands of the Eternal on the individual, has the task of preparing him for the confession that he is a long way from the ideal of self-renouncing love. At the end of the book it is obvious that the individual has come to the understanding that he stands in need of grace.

After *Works of Love* came *Christian Discourses,* which presents in four parts the ascending levels of religious development in such a manner that the last discourse talks about grace in its decisive meaning. As to the content of the four discourses, in the first Kierkegaard speaks once again of our schoolmasters—the lily and the bird—and of how we learn from the birds to relinquish all our troubled concerns. He mentions all the troubled concerns which are related to the temporal life. It is noteworthy that he begins with the purely material troubled concerns, such as "troubled concern about insufficiency and troubled concern about sufficiency; troubled concern about being unimportant and troubled concern about being important." He ascends to more spiritual concerns, such as "the troubled concern of presumption, of self-torment, of irresolution, of inconstancy, of desolation." In these reflections Kierkegaard sets before us the pagan who is concerned only about the things of this world and contrasts him with the man who by faith in God's guidance in all his life relationships can conquer the troubled concerns of this world.

The second section, "Exultant Voices in the Conflict of Suffering," deals with discipleship, and once again, to mitigate the suffering which attends it, speaks much of joy. All seven discourses in this section deal with the Christian's struggle with himself and the world, and all seven begin with the refrain: "The joy in the fact that . . ."—for example, "what you lose in temporal life you win eternally." In these discourses the two spheres—the temporal and the eternal—are placed in sharp contrast, and we see how the Christian must in his deep inward-

ness suffer through the split between time and eternity and
learn to hold fast to the Eternal. Each discourse emphasizes in
its own way the fact that all loss in the temporal world is of no
consequence compared to the loss of the hope of the Eternal
and that the only thing a man has to fear is sin, which is "man's
corruption."

The third section, "Thoughts Which Wound from Behind—
for Edification," is designed to help the individual reflect upon
his progress along the way which Christianity's requirement
has laid out for him. It says, among other things, that "the
Christian way is the way of free will"[95] and that "it is a blessed
thing to suffer the humiliation of abuse for a good purpose."[96]
One traces here Kierkegaard's own experience when he inten-
tionally exposed himself voluntarily to the *Corsair's* humiliating
attack. But he immediately warns earnestly against regarding
voluntary suffering as something worthy of merit. On the contrary, this section has the task of showing a man's helplessness
to do the good and of preparing man to accept grace. This is
abundantly clear in the words: "No, depart from me, damned
assurance! Save me, O God, from ever becoming absolutely
certain. Preserve me in the hinterland of uncertainty so that it
may always be absolutely certain that if I attain salvation I
receive it by grace."[97]

This section is extremely important because we find in the
last discourse a poetic statement of Kierkegaard's own moving
"confession of faith." It is my opinion that we have here a
description of how the transition from Religion A to Religion
B is effected. *Concluding Unscientific Postscript*[98] gives only
a theoretical survey of the transition from Religion A to Religion
B and informs us that the leap from A to B is effected when
the individual has fully realized his own insufficiency and sets
all his hope in Christ. Christ now becomes for the individual

not only the prototype but the Savior. Up until now all the edifying discourses have been a preparation for this "leap," which in the last discourse in this section, entitled "He Is Believed in the World," is described as an existential act. Here a single individual testifies that he has bound his life to this One alone and the single individual confirms this with his personal confession, "*I* have believed in him."[99] Attention is drawn to the fact that this step is not easy, that it passes through the cruel temptation which says "if"—what if, after all, this is something other than what Christ taught. This temptation is conquered by the decision to bind one's life to this One at any cost. Very earnest words are uttered in this "confession of faith," where the single individual decides to break with everything if this is demanded. "So I love many things, in different ways, in different degrees; but if He, in whom I believe, demands it of me—I will relinquish all this love for love of Him in whom I believe."[100] "For without Him it is a matter of indifference whether I live or whether I die . . . ."[101] It is clear from all this that the single individual has set all his hope in this One.

The last section, "Discourses Before Communion on Fridays," consists of seven quite short discourses which aim to prepare the individual to understand and to accept forgiveness. Christ as Savior is central in these discourses. The last one clearly states that forgiveness is unmerited. "You cannot meet Him before the altar as a co-worker in the same way as you can meet God in your daily work as a co-worker. Co-worker with Christ in the matter of atonement you cannot be, not in any possible manner. The guilt is entirely yours; the expiation is entirely His."[102] In *Christian Discourses* the doctrine of the atonement, the central thought of Christianity, is set in an existential relationship to the single individual. Kierkegaard stresses grace as the ultimate point of rest in still other discourses, which will be dealt with later.

He published *Three Godly Discourses,* where for the third time he takes up the subject of "The Lily and the Bird." In these three discourses he carries out with utmost clarity his usual method of progressively building up his presentation. The first discourse, with an aesthetic emphasis, wishes to lead man out of multiplicity that he may listen to God in silence. The second discourse, with an ethical accent, places man before the ethical Either-Or and wishes to teach him obedience to the Eternal. The third discourse emphasizes joy in the midst of all concerns as the essential factor in the religious existence. This time Kierkegaard deliberately couches "The Lily and the Bird" in nature description and gives it a more poetic color and magnificence in order to prove that the poetic must go.[103] As a result we can perhaps learn more from this little collection than from the other edifying literature of how Kierkegaard presses aesthetic means into the service of the religious.

At this time Kierkegaard is very engrossed with Christianity's last position—martyrdom. Kierkegaard, true to his singularity, had reflected earlier on his own attitude to this last level of Christianity. His conflict with the *Corsair,* the *Corsair's* ridicule of him, and his subsequent isolation and loneliness bring him existentially nearer to an understanding of the Christian's fate in the world. He struggles for clarity to understand how much will be demanded from him in this respect and how far he of his own free will should run the risk of humiliation and attack. Clarifying assistance was given to him in his pondering by the situation of a pastor from Bornholm. Pastor Adler of Hasle and Rutsker on Bornholm, a contemporary of Kierkegaard's, claimed that he had received a direct revelation from God. This claim motivated Kierkegaard to investigate thoroughly what it means for a man to receive a direct revelation. He concludes that in such a case a man becomes an instrument in the hands

of God, the consequence of which will be suffering and martyrdom.

In a splendid doctrinal and psychological study Kierkegaard
does not deny the possibility of a revelation at any time, but
he rejects Adler's claim of having had a revelation and attributes
it to mental confusion. Adler's case, however, helps Kierkegaard
to understand better his own future attitude and task. He
could not claim that he himself had had a revelation of his
mission and a direct call to "witness" about Christianity; he
does, however, feel that he has a special task to fulfill, even
though, suffering great temptations, he has had to struggle
through to new decisions. The case of Adler, therefore, touches
Kierkegaard's own tender spot. In *The Book on Adler,* which
is in his *Journals,* Kierkegaard writes very cogently on the problem of a special calling from God. He published only a part of
it as *Two Minor Ethico-Religious Treatises,* which deal with
the subjects: "Has a man a right to let himself be killed for the
sake of truth?" and "Of the difference between a genius and
an apostle."

The result of Kierkegaard's reflections is that he does not
regard himself as being called "to witness" in a crucial sense—
he is too much of a "poet." It becomes very clear to Kierkegaard that he can only relate himself to the last position in
Christianity as one relates to an ideal before which one must
be humbled. He understands that his strength lies in the rapture
of the Christian ideal and his ability to depict Christianity in
its true form. The boundary of how far he should venture is
now assigned. The ideal of martyrdom, which has drawn him
since his youth, is ever before him—but only as an ideal.
Until now he has tested all the other levels of religious development in his own experience; he has the right to sign his name
to them. To the last one, which is described in *Training in*

*Christianity,* he signs a pseudonym so that he may honestly designate the distance between his own life and the ideal which he sets forth in the book.

*Training in Christianity* consists of three sections, each introduced by a verse from the Gospels which is repeated often and is the keynote for that particular section. In this book all the Christian definitions and concepts are applied existentially— words like *contemporaneity, offense,* and *belief,* which he had already introduced in *Philosophical Fragments.* In the first part of the book we hear the words from the Gospel: "Come unto me, all ye who are heavy laden, and I will give you rest." We are invited to meet Christ as one very near to us and to experience what it means to be contemporary with him. *Philosophical Fragments* prepared the way for an understanding of what is meant by contemporaneity. This book elaborates on the fact that it was just as difficult for Christ's contemporaries to believe in him as it is for later generations. The incarnation of Christ contains a contradiction for logical thought—the contradiction being this, that a man, subject to all the laws of corruption, claims to be God. Christ's contemporaries, as well as later generations, could accept Christ as the Son of God only with the eyes of faith. When Christ came into the world, he was "a sign of contradiction," and this he will be for all time.

One must not let himself be helped into Christianity, either, by the deception that because Christianity has existed for such a long time there must be some truth in it. Since Christianity involves a logical contradiction, the absurd (the incarnation), we may not use history to make the truth of Christianity probable. From a philosophical point of view, Christianity is absurd; from a historical point of view, it is improbable. The book asserts that we may easily be convinced of this if we think of ourselves as contemporary with Christ. One will then discover that "Christ is the paradox, the object of faith, existing only for faith."[104] To support this assertion the book brings Christ to nineteenth century Copenhagen and shows how he would be subjected to the same suffering and humiliation as when he lived among Jews, even though there is a church there which is called Christian. Through his pseudonym, Kierkegaard lets different classes of society express their opinion about this Christ who is making a disturbance in the streets. Everywhere he creates annoyance and offense. Most people will not have anything to do with him. Only a few poor people join him—but they, of course, have nothing to lose.

Of the many condemnations and attacks made by these representatives of the different classes of society, the one made by the solid citizen is here quoted: "No, let us be men!"

The average is good enough. Too little and too much spoil everything, and, as a French proverb which I heard from a traveling salesman says, all excessiveness will eventually go bankrupt. This man is doomed for sure. I have spoken very severely to my son about him, warned him and lectured him about going to the dogs and joining up with this man. Why? Because all run after him. Yes, and who are they? Unemployed reprobates, vagabonds, and tramps—who run after anybody. Not many solid, well-off people, and none of the good, decent people by whom I always set my watch—not City Councilman Jeppesen nor Councilman Marchus nor the rich merchant Christophersen. No, these people know what's what. And if we look at the clergy who understand these things best—they won't have anything to do with him. It was Pastor Greenwold himself who said last evening at the Club, "That life will end in something terrible," and that fellow knows something more than just preaching. You ought not listen to him Sundays in the church but Mondays at the Club. I wish I had half of his understanding of the world. He was perfectly right—he took the words out of my mouth—when he said, "It's only loose and idle people who run after him."[105]

Christ's appearance in Copenhagen is an open attack on the church, which has flattened out and has conformed itself to the world.

The second part of *Training in Christianity* explains what decisions the individual must make when he becomes contemporary with Christ and when he is asked about his relationship to the Man who has called him. There are only two ways one can relate himself to Christ—either in faith in him or in offense at him. We are reminded of this last possibility by the Bible verse which is the theme of the second part of the book: "Blessed is he who shall not be offended in me" (Matt. 11:6). The possibility of offense in relation to belief is defined thus: "Just as the concept *faith* is a very essential characteristic of Christianity, so *offense* is also an essential characteristic of Christianity and is related to faith. The possibility of offense is the crossroads or is similar to standing at the crossroads. One swings from the possibility of offense either to offense itself or to faith, but one never comes to faith except from the possibility of offense."[106]

Three different kinds of offense are set forth. The first concerns Christ as a great man. One is offended by the news which he brings. Any great man can occasion this kind of offense by the collision of his revolutionary ideas with the traditional ones. This is not especially characteristic of Christ. The Pharisees' offense belongs to this class. They did not believe Christ to be God, but still they were offended because Christ would abolish their traditions. The two other kinds of offense are related to faith in Christ as the Son of God. Kierkegaard calls one of them the offense of eminence and the other the offense of lowliness.

The possibility of the offense of eminence comes about when one confronts the fact that a single individual out and out behaves as if he were God.

He defines himself in such a superhumanly spiritual way that he speaks of eating his flesh and drinking his blood, a statement which leans as fantastically as possible toward the divine attribute of omnipresence, and yet again as paradoxically as possible in that it is his flesh and blood. He says that only that one who eats his body and drinks his blood will he raise up at the last day—certainly defining himself as God in the most decisive expressions! He says that he is the bread which comes down from heaven—again a decisive expression in the direction of divinity. And when he knew that his disciples growled about this and found it hard to take he says, "Does this offend you?" and then follows the still stronger expression, "What if you then shall see the Son of Man ascend up where he was before?" Consequently, far from yielding or minimizing himself, he straightforwardly makes himself out to be something entirely different from a human being; he makes himself out to be divine—he, a simple man![107]

One is tempted by such conduct on the part of Christ to regard him as a blasphemer. When one is contemporary with him it is possible to believe these words only by being helped to risk the leap of faith. It is very easy to imagine that one is a believer from a distance.

In the next form of offense, the offense of lowliness, man begins with the supposition that Christ is the Son of God but is brought to a standstill by his lowliness and impotence. "He is the God-man, and one is offended that he is debased in this way."[108] This is the strongest form of offense; not even Christ's disciples can escape it. "The disciples, who had believed in his divinity and in this respect had bypassed the possibility of offense in that direction by becoming believers, were brought to a standstill by his lowliness, by the possibility of offense which lies in the fact that the God-man suffers in every way as one merely human."[109] A moment came when they were all offended in him. They could not continue to believe in Christ as God when they saw his defeat and his defenselessness before his enemies. That kind of ecclesiastical mentality which regards itself as quite secure against offense appears ridiculous when even the disciples of the Lord failed him at the critical moment.

In the second part of *Training in Christianity* the difference between the pagan and the Christian understanding of truth is also treated. In paganism truth is a doctrine, and the person is less important than the doctrine; in Christianity the opposite is true. Here it is the person, Christ, who is truth itself and "Christ [is] infinitely more important that his doctrine."[110] Relevant to this difference between the pagan sages and Christ, Kierkegaard explains why Christ could never communicate with anyone in a direct way.

> When One says directly, "I am God—the Father and I are one," this is a direct communication. But when he who says this, the communicator, is a plain human being like everybody else, then this is not entirely direct communication; for it is not entirely direct that a plain human being should be God, although what he says is perfectly direct. The communication contains a contradiction, because of him who communicates the communication becomes indirect communication. It places before one the choice of believing him or not believing him.[111]

Consequently, Christ places man before an absolute decision, with the possibility of salvation or of damnation, but he cannot himself communicate directly to anyone. Kierkegaard develops further that "the impossibility of simple, direct communication is the secret of Christ's suffering."[112]

The third part of *Training in Christianity,* containing seven discourses, is essentially concerned with discipleship. The theme for this portion is given in the verse from the Gospel: "And when I am lifted up from the earth I will draw all men to myself." A description of Kierkegaard's own rapture is interwoven into these reflections of how Christ draws an individual to himself. Without a doubt, a portion of the third and fourth discourses is autobiographical. We see here how a child is affected by a vigorously religious atmosphere, how he cannot forget the treatment which Christ received in the world, how the figure of the Crucified One becomes the ideal of his youthful longing, how without relinquishing the ideal he comes deeper and deeper into suffering. All this is an account of the ideal which attracts Kierkegaard.

This portion of *Training in Christianity* also stresses the fact that Christian truth is not a conclusion or a system—but a way. Only by living according to it does it become a reality for a person. Free will is again accented as being distinctly Christian. A distinction is drawn between unavoidable suffering and the suffering to which a man exposes himself out of free decision. Only the latter is Christian suffering. From the demand for discipleship the discussion leads as a matter of course to the subject of the battling church as a characteristic of early Christianity. With this as a criterion, the book launches into an attack on the contemporary church. In the conclusion of the book the difference between an admirer and a disciple is drawn. Christianity's demand is discipleship and not admiration. "Only the disciple is the true Christian,"[113] it declares.

In *Training in Christianity* the climax of the Christian demands is reached. Martyrdom is set forth as the highest point on the Christian way. With martyrdom the ranking of values is complete. Against the disintegration of values which he has fought from the very beginning, Kierkegaard affirms a scale of values on which the Christian martyr ranks the highest.* With the martyr the last degree of the synthesis of the temporal and the Eternal is reached. At this point man with his temporal desires recedes and becomes completely God's instrument.

The whole edifying literature which we have just examined reveals how the Eternal, the dominant force of the synthesis, gets increasing power over man. *The Sickness unto Death,* pub-

---

*A man must always have a prototype, so the question is not whether or not one chooses a prototype but which prototype one chooses. Kirkegaard introduces the martyr as a prototype not merely for the sake of imitation but first and foremost as an ideal which judges us by its high demand. We must remember here also that Kierkegaard speaks very clearly against "the ascetic fanaticism" which forgets that "God is the God of patience" (*Pap.* X², A 241).

lished in 1849, almost a year before *Training in Christianity*, is the counterpart to this positive emphasis in the edifying literature. *Sickness unto Death* describes the disrelationship between the two components of the synthesis, the Eternal and the temporal. While the rest of the edifying literature deals with man's progress on the way of faith, Kierkegaard in *The Sickness unto Death* describes in mounting succession man's attempts to break away from faith. The condition of the man without faith is one of despair and offense. The highest form of offense is to declare, against one's better convictions, that "Christianity is untrue and a lie. This form of offense is a sin against the Holy Spirit."[14] In *Training in Christianity* and *The Sickness unto Death* the most extreme contrasts possible in a man's religious positions are achieved—on the one side one who has become an instrument of God and on the other the conscious rebel against God.

It may not be necessary, perhaps, to point out that Kierkegaard considers the possibilities of despair and offense as described in *The Sickness unto Death* to be ever-present dangers for man, and that only faith can help us to conquer them every time. The *Sickness unto Death* illustrates rather well Kierkegaard's ability to build a whole scale of human postures and positions from a single sentence about the synthesis.

The edifying literature comes to a close with *Two Discourses at the Communion on Friday* (1851), in which Kierkegaard strongly emphasizes grace. These discourses are introduced by the following confession:

An authorship begun in *Either-Or* and progressing by stages comes to rest finally at the foot of the altar, where the author, conscious of his own imperfection and guilt, by no means calls himself a witness of the truth but only a special kind of poet and thinker who "without authority" has produced nothing new but has wished to read the primitive document about individual, human, existential relationships, the old familiar writings transmitted from our fathers, to read them again, if possible, in a more inward manner.[115]

In these discourses grace ranks highest among what is essentially Christian, and Kierkegaard lets himself be judged by the ideal he sets forth.

In his edifying literature Kierkegaard has charted the ethical-religious way in progress and in decline. For him Christianity is not a system or a dogma far removed from life but the Life and the Way itself, and that is why there are so many levels in the growth of inwardness or in the flight from inwardness.

Having described the religious way and having found the highest form of Christianity in the militant early church, Kierkegaard, using this as his standard, turns his attention in *For Self-Examination* and *Judge for Yourself* to contemporary conditions and indicates the cleft between the militant church of old and the ecclesiastical mentality of the present church. Of these closely related books, he himself published only *For Self-Examination*. *Judge for Yourself* was published after Kierkegaard's death by his brother. Consequently, the tone of both of these books is openly polemic.

In reviewing these two collections of discourses, I would draw attention especially to the last meditation in *For Self-Examination*, which is about the Holy Spirit, who guides to the Truth and the Life. The Holy Spirit is like the royal coachman who drives his horses in the proper manner. But now men are guided by other spirits, and driving is badly done. It is once more necessary for the royal coachman to take the reins and the lead as he did of old with the Christians of the first century. We read:

When I think of myself and the countless people I have learned to know, I have often said to myself in sadness: "Here are capacities and powers and possibilities enough—but the driver is lacking." Through the long ages, for generation after generation, we human beings have been driven, if I may say so, according to the horses' conception of driving. We have been governed, trained, and educated according to man's conception of what it is to be a man. You see what has come from that—we lack spiritual stature. It follows from this again that we can endure so little, that we impatiently use the means of the moment, impatiently wait to see instantaneous rewards for our labors, which for this very reason become of secondary importance. Once it was otherwise. There was a time when it pleased the Deity Himself, if I may say so, to be the coachman, and He drove the horses according to a coachman's conception of what driving is. What was man not capable of then![116]

Kierkegaard did not publish any more books after *For Self-Examination,* but he wrote copiously in his *Journals.* He expected now some sort of admission from the official church, especially from Bishop Mynster. Certainly, if it had come, his authorship would have had a less tragic end. However, nobody took him seriously but at the most considered him a disagreeable disturber of the peace. Kierkegaard prepared himself for the possibility of having to set an emphatic conclusion to his whole authorship if the admission did not come. From his *Journals* it is evident that he reckoned with several possibilities and had everything in readiness if he should have to launch an attack on the church. His veneration for Bishop Mynster restrained him, but one senses the difficulty of his dilemma. The opportune moment drew near when Bishop Mynster died and the future bishop, Martensen, conducted the burial service and called Bishop Mynster one of the "witnesses of the truth who like a holy chain stretch from the day of the apostles through the ages." Kierkegaard, who had just described what it is to be a "witness of the Truth" in his most recent writings, realized that the moment for calling an "alarm" was at hand. He waited, however, until Professor Martensen had been appointed bishop, but then began his violent attack.

Kierkegaard's writings during the attack fill a whole volume in addition to the running commentary in the *Journals*. Without this attack the authorship would lack the factor of offense which is necessary when a new and decisive point of view is to be put forward. The attack is like the dot over the *i* in his authorship. It is so sharply worded that it must result either in offense or in reflection and an awakening.

At the time when Kierkegaard fell down in the street, during the conflict with the church, he had accomplished the task which the "Governing Power" had assigned to him.

This short survey of Kierkegaard's total authorship has tried to trace the principal direction of his writing. It must be admitted that there are many significant points which have not even been mentioned. In self-defense, the author reminds the reader that Kierkegaard, starting from his theory, takes positions with regard to all sides of human existence, with the result that there are plenty of problems and problem solutions in his books as well as in his *Journals!* But just like the theory of the stages, all of Kierkegaard's other reflections rest upon the basic concept about man as a synthesis of the Eternal and the temporal. It is Kierkegaard's great service to show how only this Christian premise is adequate enough to illuminate and to bring meaning to the numerous problematic situations of human existence. This basic concept from which Christianity proceeds will certainly show itself to be superior to all other interpretations of man, for only Christianity sees truly into the depths and the heights of man. As we have seen, the synthesis-formulation helps Kierkegaard to get a comprehensive view of all sides of human existence, just as it also influences the working out of his theories on immortality, dialectical freedom, and the communication of the truth—all of which play an essential role in his authorship.

# V. *The Problems of the Self and Immortality*

In his authorship Søren Kierkegaard (or his pseudonyms) discusses three groups of problems as being especially difficult. A note in his *Journals* declares that the problem of freedom and motion "is perhaps one of the most difficult problems in all philosophy."[117] It is well known that reflections about freedom are central in Kierkegaard's thought.

The next group of especially difficult questions is concerned with the implications of the Christ-relationship to the situations of human life. At this point, says Kierkegaard, "we meet by far the most difficult of all problems."* He tries then to clarify these difficulties, for this very problem of Christ as "prototype" plays a decisive role in his understanding of Christianity.

The third group of problems, which Kierkegaard's pseudonyms Vigilius Haufniensis and Johannes Climacus both regard

---

*I have attempted to show the significance the question about Christ as "prototype" had for Kierkegaard in my article "Søren Kierkegaards Modifikationer af det kristelige" in *Dansk teologisk Tidsskrift* 20, 1957 (See *Pap.* IV A, 62, also A 47, A 103).

as extremely difficult, concerns the question of how a particular human being becomes a self, or in what sense one can talk about individual immortality (in Kierkegaard's mind these terms mean the same). It is on this subject we would now focus the reader's attention.

The problem itself can be stated in this way: Both pseudonymous authors start from the presupposition that every man has the possibility of the Eternal within himself—but only as a possibility. Not until there is a transition from possibility to actuality—a transition which gives man a new quality—can there be in any real sense talk of individual immortality and of a man's becoming a self. Previous to the transition, a man is simply a particular being characterized by the fact that his race is ultimate. The whole of a man's existence still lies within the scheme of temporality and is submerged in the process of world history.

These problems are clearly expressed by Vigilius Haufniensis as well as by Johannes Climacus. Haufniensis writes: "Every human being is intended for the religious life. To want to deny this is to confuse the issues and to abolish the concept of individual, race, and immortality. At this point one wishes for keen discernment, for here indeed are very difficult problems."[118]

Concerning "world history" and its relation to the individual and the race, Johannes Climacus makes the following statement in *Concluding Unscientific Postscript:* "If world history is anything at all, it must be the history of the race. Now here is a problem which in my opinion is one of the most difficult. How and to what extent does race result from individuals, and what is the relationship of individuals to the race?"[119]

Before going deeper into the quandaries posed in these two statements, one should note two things. In the first place, one should observe that it is Kierkegaard's pseudonymous authors

—the psychologist Vigilius Haufniensis and the dialectician Johannes Climacus—who talk about the difficulties of this question. Why Kierkegaard did not introduce these reflections in the beginning under his own name but waited to do it much later in his *Journals* will subsequently become apparent.

In the second place, it must be noted once again that in Kierkegaard's authorship the question of individual immortality is intimately bound up with reflections on the becoming of a self and thereby to the concept of "the single individual" *(den Enkelte)*. Only when he has come into an existential relationship to the Eternal and has made the leap from the possibility of the Eternal to the actuality of the Eternal is a human being qualified as a self or as a single individual. We may therefore consider the concepts of immortality, the self, and the single solitary individual as parallel concepts. Since Kierkegaard has treated the concept of self very completely and comprehensively, we will pay particular attention to it in this study.

With these two points in mind, let us now look more closely at the difficulties about which both pseudonymous authors speak.

When one considers the relationship between the particular human being, race, and immortality, one understands that it is difficult to support the idea of individual immortality in those cases where the individual is only an instance in the life of the race. In the beginning of his life, every human being is this, for each one always begins his life related first and foremost to the race, and as such is a transient instance. In this sense, then, it becomes meaningless to talk about individual immortality.

The difficulties are sharpened still more by the fact that while throwing light upon these problems Kierkegaard works with two presuppositions which in certain places seem to contradict each other.

One of these presuppositions—which can be termed the dog-

matic one—declares that all men are immortal.* This is the
unshakable point of departure in Kierkegaard's view of man.
He never departs from it or lets his pseudonyms depart from it.
This presupposition is a declaration of man's essential being
quite apart from his historical development—that is, in Kierkegaardian language—still apart from the existential development. This presupposition coincides with Kierkegaard's thesis
about man as a synthesis of time and the Eternal.

The second presupposition concerns the existential, which
unquestionably is decisive in Kierkegaard's thought. The statement that all men are immortal holds only in the abstract. This
"abstract definition"[120] first obtains concrete meaning along
with the existential presupposition. With this, the statement
that man is a synthesis of the temporal and the Eternal and
thereby immortal, acquires a different significance, depending
entirely on the level of existence where man finds himself.

On the lower level of existence it can seem as if the statement about the synthesis, which asserts that man has the
Eternal within himself, is meaningless, for when the Eternal
in man is not actualized and man does not become a self, man
does not become immortal, even if he is intended for immortality. On the other hand, it must be said that if man does not
have the Eternal within himself, the existential line cannot be
carried through. The first is the condition for the existential
development. Consequently, these two trains of thought must
be affirmed, even when by intensive reflection one discovers a
contradictory relationship between them. On the one hand one
attributes to the particular human being the possibility of immortality, but on the other hand one makes the actualization
of the possibility dependent upon existence. If the particular

---

*Kierkegaard's views on the relationship between immortality and resurrection
will be touched upon later.

human being's existence is completely absorbed in the race's universally historical process, this possibility is not actualized.* The consequence of this, then, is that there can be instances in which immortal man actually does not become immortal in his personal existence. However, every man has the possibility of the Eternal within himself. Can this possibility be lost once it has been given? With this question, we are deep in "one of the most difficult of all" problems.

In a short section of *Concluding Unscientific Postscript* entitled "On Being Immortal"[121] Climacus probes deeper into all the difficulties which accompany the question about immortality. In his delineation of the problem he stresses punctiliously the existential line. Climacus knows that to pronounce dogmas on the immortality of the soul leads nowhere since the question must be solved in such a way that existence itself is involved. Probingly, Climacus raises many questions about immortality, but in answering the question about what it means to be immortal, he himself employs only existential considerations. Immortality is for him "subjectivity developed and raised to its highest level."[122] He can also define immortality as "the eternal identity with oneself," which is precisely the criterion for spirit and, thereby, for the self. It is clearly apparent here that Climacus wants to throw some doubt on the assertion that all men are immortal.

In stressing the significance of existence for immortality, Climacus takes sharp issue with the frivolousness with which immortality is sometimes treated. By generalizing immortality

---

*In *Fear and Trembling* Johannes the Silent sketches the whole problematic relationship between the particular human being and the race. Examples are given of the relationship in which the particular human being is subordinated to the race ("the universal") and also in which the single individual in the power of his relationship to the Eternal becomes "higher than the universal" (*S.V.* III, p. 115; *Fear and Trembling,* p. 100).

into something universal one demonstrates that he does not comprehend the problem at all. Climacus says further,

> The question about immortality is fantastically made into a joke, just as the opposite situation is a joke—namely, that people who have fantastically botched everything and have been everything possible somehow get anxious one fine day and ask the minister whether they really will be the same in the next world—after being incapable in life of remaining the same for two weeks and therefore having experienced all sorts of changes. Immortality, then, would certainly be a remarkable metamorphosis if it could change such an unhuman centipede into an eternal identity with itself, which is what "being the same" really is.[123]

Regarding the one who relates himself in the right manner to the thought of immortality, Climacus says:

> To ask about his immortality, moreover, is certainly for the existing subject who asks the question an act, something it positively is not for those distracted people who vaguely ask now and then about this matter of being immortal, as if being immortal were something one is once in a while and the questioner were something in general. So he asks how to go about expressing immortality in his existing, whether he really is expressing it, and for the present he is satisfied with this task, which must easily last for a lifetime since it is to last for eternity.[124]

Climacus knows very well that stressing the existential will probably come in conflict with certain interpretations of such passages in Scripture as Matthew 19:14: "Suffer the little children to come to me, and forbid them not, for of such is the kingdom of heaven." Consequently, it is quite appropriate that he defends his unique interpretation of this quotation from the New Testament in one of the last chapters of *Concluding Unscientific Postscript*.[125]

But at the same time that Kierkegaard emphasizes through his pseudonyms the significance of existence for immortality, other emphases may occasionally be heard. In isolated portions it may seem as if the existential is not being considered, as when

Kierkegaard in a *Journal* entry in 1847 speaks about "the irony and the earnestness" which are present in the following statement: "We are all immortal. If someone immerses himself completely in this thought and lives into it, he does not thereby become more immortal than all of us are."[126]

We must not forget that these two lines of thinking—the dogmatic and the existential—come into conflict only on the lower levels of human existence, there where man has not yet come to know the Eternal and therefore does not have the possibility of realizing it. The relationship between these two lines of thought is something else when we assume that man has encountered the Eternal in his existence. Then the thesis that man is immortal means it acutally is so for him. The dogmatic presupposition then receives its verification in existence.

In *The Sickness unto Death* the pseudonymous Anti-Climacus gives a detailed dialectical description of man's becoming a self and of the stages in the actualization of the self. Only through these stages in the coming into existence of the self does the synthesis of man find its real meaning. Spirit, the self, is the "positive third" which binds the two elements of the synthesis into a unity. Previously there was only a "negative unity." The difference between negative and positive unity is studied in the two books *The Concept of Anxiety* and *The Sickness unto Death*. In *The Concept of Anxiety* the unity between the two elements of the synthesis is still only negative, for the movement is still mainly within the qualification body-soul, only approximating spirit, the self. Not until *The Sickness unto Death* do we find characterizations of "the positive third, and this is the self."[127]

The description of the coming into existence of the self in *The Sickness unto Death* is broadened to a dialectical survey of all the stages of the self, considered under the qualification of sin. In addition to this detailed survey of the dialectic of the self, we find brief outlines which indicate the self's dialectical transitions. Especially in the chapter "Gradations in the Consciousness of the Self"[128] do we find such an outline. In shortened form the outline appears thus: First there is "unconsciousness of having an eternal self"; after that, in definite gradations, "knowledge of having a self in which there is something eternal." This self, says Anti-Climacus, is still "within the definition of the human self, or the self whose measure is man." "But," continues Anti-Climacus, "this self gets a new quality and qualification through being the self directly before God. This self is no longer a merely human self but is what I, hoping not to be misunderstood, would call the theological self, the self directly before God. What infinite reality the self receives by being conscious of existing before God, by becoming a human self whose measure is God!"

Anti-Climacus then gives examples of how "the self rises to its highest potential in relation to the measure before the self, and infinitely when God is the measure." Regarding paganism, he says, "The pagan did not have his self directly before God. The pagan and the natural man have merely the human self as their measure."[129]

The self reaches its highest potential in the encounter with the revealed truth, Christ. In Anti-Climacus' own words:

A self directly before Christ is a self potentiated by the enormous gift of God, potentiated by the enormous significance which is placed on him by the fact that God, for the sake of this self also, let himself be born, become man, suffered, and died. The greater the apprehension of God, the greater the self; likewise it is true that the greater the apprehension of Christ, the greater the self. That Christ is the measure is a divinely attested expression of the vast reality a self has, for only in Christ is it true that God is man's goal and measure, or measure and goal.[130]

The outline for the dialectic of the self in *The Sickness unto Death* is made without considering whether man is moving along the way of faith, despair, or offense. But *The Sickness unto Death* as a whole, on the basis of this outline, concentrates on showing how the self potentiates its despair, and later offense, through its opposition to the progressive realization of the synthesis. The presentation of the gradations of self in *The Sickness unto Death* may therefore rightly be called "the dialectic of sin," a phrase Anti-Climacus himself uses two times.[131] How the self comes to life on the way of faith, the reverse of sin, Kierkegaard develops in his edifying works, especially in *Training in Christianity* under the pseudonym Anti-Climacus. This book can be considered a counterpart to *The Sickness unto Death*.

Almost everything touched upon so far is taken from the discourses of the pseudonymous writers. They, especially the lower-stage pseudonymous writers who preceded Anti-Climacus, venture to present the problem of the self and immortality for scrutiny. It is otherwise with Kierkegaard as an edifying author. An edifying author makes men aware of God and the Eternal, but in doing this he makes them captive within the self's coming-into-existence. A man becomes a self responsible to the Eternal when he is placed before the decision at which *The Edifying Discourses* point. Whether man is positive or negative to the demands, he still remains a self. The religious speaker does not have the same difficulties as the one who wants to clarify intellectually the problem of the self and immortality. His only task is to call man's attention to the Eternal.[132]

After this Kierkegaard uses in the service of religion the format for the dialectic of the self and the insight into the problem of immortality which he has acquired as a thinker. Mention is made here of only one discourse (1843), "Need of

God Is Man's Highest Perfection." This speaks very clearly of the self's coming into existence, of how "a man's true self," his "deeper self," begins to struggle with the "first self," which is man's body-soul synthesis and which binds man to the external world with all its possibilities. Using the dialectic of the self, Kierkegaard illustrates further the religious truth that "by himself man cannot conquer himself."[133]

In the domain of the religious, the difficulties are no longer to be found in comprehending and harmonizing ideas but in actualizing the given presuppositions concerning the soul's immortality and the self. This is especially clear in a sermon from *Christian Discourses* entitled "There will be a Resurrection of the Dead—both of the Righteous—and of the Unrighteous."[134] The difference between mere speculation about immortality and the existential earnestness which ought to stamp thinking about immortality is of direct concern in this discourse. Kierkegaard says here, "When immortality becomes a question, then God is abolished and the race is god."[135] Instead of talking about the possible proofs for the immortality of the soul, the religious speaker uses a completely different language. He says, "Do not doubt that you are immortal. Tremble that you are immortal!"[136]

Because he is immortal, man is responsible for his life. Therefore Kierkegaard can say further, "Immortality is the judgment." The man who has heard of this is made captive in a great responsibility which he no longer can escape, and the religious discourse would say to him: "You are immortal, and you must make an accounting to God, immortal one, of how you have lived! Precisely because you are immortal you will not be able to escape from God; you will not be able to mislay yourself in a grave and appear as if nothing were the matter, and the measure by which you will be judged by God is this— that you are immortal."[137]

These are completely different tones than those used in the survey of the different dialectical aspects of immortality and the self. It is worth noticing that Kierkegaard here places the idea of the immortality of the soul together with faith in the resurrection. To Paul's words in Acts 24:15: *"There will be a resurrection of the dead—both of the righteous—and of the unrighteous"* Kierkegaard appends the following, with the same underscoring: "or *about the proof for the immortality of the soul, the answer is this—it is only all too certain. Fear it!"*[138]

Kierkegaard speaks very often about immortality but only in a few places about the resurrection, which he links to immortality. This shows that Kierkegaard would not agree with those who maintain that immortality and resurrection are two sharply conflicting ideas. As far as I can judge, immortality and resurrection in Kierkegaard's thought stand in the following relationship to each other: immortality lies on another plane— one could say on a lower one—than resurrection. Immortality signifies, in the first place, as we have seen, that possibility for the Eternal which is common to all men, Greeks and Jews.* It is clear that for Kierkegaard this possibility does not become a genuine reality until it is related to God. One can therefore legitimately speak of a man's immortality even in this life. Not so with resurrection, which lies on another plane and is connected with the restoration of all things. The resurrection faith always looks toward a future, whereas faith in immortality is grounded in God's creative act, by which every man as a synthesis of time and the Eternal has received the possibility of the Eternal in himself; the resurrection is connected with salvation

---

*Kierkegaard firmly believed that with Socrates the Greeks approached the possibility of immortality as "recollection." Judaism, too, held that God set the Eternal in the hearts of men (Ecclesiastes 3:11). For a more profound analysis of this verse see Kierkegaard (*S.V.* VIII, pp. 122 ff.; *Purity of Heart*, p. 36 ff.).

through Christ and his promise of eternal life. On this basis it is impossible for immortality and resurrection ever to come in opposition to each other in Kierkegaard. This also explains why on previously mentioned occasions he places immortality and resurrection in relation to each other. For Kierkegaard it is clear as day that only a being who has the possibility of immortality within himself, and who in relationship to God receives the possibility of individual immortality, can rise again to an eternal life.

From all this we can see that the question of immortality and the self is simplified for Kierkegaard as a religious author. Immortality and judgment stand fast, it must be affirmed, and the single individual must under his own responsibility take his position in relation to them. In this sense it can be said that "one of the most difficult" problems finds its solution in the Christian-religious area. It is no longer a problem but a work of proclamation.

At the same time it is noteworthy that the later Kierkegaard, the Kierkegaard who molded weapons for the battle with the church, returns in his *Journals* to the same observations as Climacus made. It becomes clear to Kierkegaard that in spite of the flow of Christian words, men in Christendom live on pagan or Jewish foundations, with the race supreme. He gradually comes to the idea that it is the clergy's preaching which prevents men from deeper encounter and decision in respect to the Eternal. This is the reason why the particular human being never gets so far into existence that he is confronted by incitement toward decision to become a single individual, to become a self.

In *The Point of View for My Work as an Author* (1848), Kierkegaard writes that only a few in every generation end "with the qualification of spirit."[139] Most men only serve out time in the body-soul synthesis. They never succeed in becoming a self, and the Eternal is for them only an abstract possibility. This pessimistic view certainly became stronger through the years, and it forced him into new reflections on the individual, the race, and immortality.

For a better understanding of Kierkegaard's dialectical point of departure for these reflections, it should be stated that in his whole authorship Kierkegaard insists that there are definite tokens which show how close a man really comes to the Eternal and how far along he is on the way to becoming a self. The "movement of infinity" is among these tokens. Kierkegaard is of the opinion that only by "the movement of infinity" can a man gain the awareness of his own personal immortality. As early as *Either-Or* the movement of repentance, which is one of the forms of "the movement of infinity," is mentioned as a condition for becoming a self. Judge William finds his eternal self by repenting himself out of rootage in temporality.[140] Later we find these words of Johannes the Silent: "One can amuse himself by pondering the curious fact that precisely in the very age when everyone can achieve the very highest, doubt about the immortality of the soul is so widespread; for he who really has made only the movement of infinity can hardly doubt."[141] In these words we find not only the claim that doubt about the immortality of the soul is widespread but also the indication of the way which leads to a conviction about personal immortality. The "movement of infinity" is this way.

Kierkegaard refers to several gradations of "the movement of infinity"—such as irony, humor, resignation, and repentance. Through all of these man can reach a conviction about the reality of the Eternal. It is important to pay attention to the fact that while he was getting ready to do battle with the church Kierkegaard named the most rigorous form of "the movement

of infinity"—namely, *to die to the world.* This form of "the
movement of infinity" is now used as the measure of a man's
becoming a self, becoming immortal. Yet only the individual
man knows within himself whether he has made "the movement
of infinity."

Kierkegaard takes out this rigorous measuring stick in earnest
in 1851, and as his dissatisfaction with the ecclesiastical situation grows, he uses it to point out the far-reaching consequences
of the problem of the individual, race, and immortality. In a
*Journal* note from 1851 under the heading "Immortality," he
writes:

> Cicero says [in *De Natura Deorum,* Book II, toward the end] that
> the gods have no superiority over men except that they have immortality,
> *but this is not necessary for leading a happy life.*
> To be sure, it is very confusing the way people in Christendom force
> immortality onto men, making them believe that they feel a deep need
> for immortality.
> After all, didn't immortality first come with Christianity—and why?
> Because immortality demands that one must die to the world. To be
> able to die to the world—the Eternal and immortality must stand fast.
> Immortality and dying to the world are correlatives. In the suffering
> of dying to the world the hope of the infinite is born. But in Christen-
> dom men will cheat to get everything—immortality as well![142]

More and more, to die to the world means for Kierkegaard the
constant battle of the spirit against sensuousness. It is clear to
him that the strongest resistance to the mounting demands of the
spirit comes from the domain of sex. It is quite understandable,
therefore, why this area becomes the most important object of
his sharp attack. Kierkegaard comes to regard the sexual life
and sexuality in its wider consequences as the greatest obstacle
on the way to becoming a self. Sex is attacked on two grounds:
first, because Kierkegaard considers it an expression of the
greatest human egotism; second, because by means of sex the
individual can go entirely over into the service of the race.

Concerning these two obstacles Kierkegaard says, among other things, "Just as the nerve endings lie under the nail, so human egotism is concentrated around the sex relationship, the propagation of the race, the giving of life." He says further, "Sexuality is the culmination of human egotism."[143] This last sharp utterance says virtually the same as Vigilius Haufniensis says in his definition of sexuality, which characterizes sex as "the farthest reach of one extreme of the synthesis" or "the utmost in sensuousness." This definition now gets a purely ethical coloring.

At this time Kierkegaard looks to different authors for support for his claim that sex and the propagation of the race are an obstacle in attaining immortality. Significantly, Kierkegaard reads eagerly Friedrich Böhringer's *Die Kirche Christi und ihre Zeugen,** in which he searches the church fathers to find corroboration for these far-reaching implications.

The following *Journal* note shows his efforts in this direction:

> In addition to the drive and [everything] related to it which can propel a man into marriage, there is another consideration which I want to emphasize here. I find the same thing expressed in Plato and Aristotle and also in the church fathers [it is stated in Böhringer occasionally and is marked in my copy]: that leaving progeny is a substitute for individual immortality; therefore a man who clings tenaciously to life and does accept his immortality strives to prolong his life by leaving a family.[144]

In a previously cited note (*Journals,* XI² A 154) there is also this statement about the propagation of the race as a substitute for immortality:

> This matter about sex being the center of human egotism God, of course, knows only too well, and therefore the charge is laid here. Even

---

*Friedrich Böhringer: *Die Kirche Christi und ihre Zeugen oder die Kirchengeschichte in Biographieen*. Kierkegaard owned Volumes I-VII of this work, which was published in Zurich, 1842—1855.

the most trivial observation can easily verify that here human egotism is concentrated.

So God demanded: forsake this egotism, and then God manifested immortality. For—as I have often written (both Plato and Aristotle distinctly express it)—in paganism and Judaism propagation of the race was the substitute for immortality.

For the most part Kierkegaard arrives at the same conclusions as another modern author, Ludwig Feuerbach, whom Kierkegaard ranks high as the theologian of offense. In his work *Das Wesen des Christenthums,* Feuerbach maintains that in paganism the individual is sacrificed for the race; Christianity, on the other hand, sacrifices the race for the individual. Feuerbach also introduces the view that in paganism there is immortality only in the perpetuation of the life of the race.*

In Kierkegaard's strong statements we observe that he is wounded by the frivolousness with which men increasingly regard immortality. Among other things he says of this:

Once immortality was the high goal of the greatest possible effort, relating itself to a complete character-transformation in one's life. Now, if males and females merely copulate—there immediately results an immortal creature, and with a drop of water on the head—a Christian, with the expectation of eternal blessedness.

Would this not, after all, be all too cheap a way to produce immortal works?

In Christendom Christianity, which is spirit, is changed to brutishness and animality.

And so it goes on—. No one suspects anything. Everyone thinks the whole business is wonderful.[145]

It is evident that Kierkegaard strongly rejects the idea of universal salvation. Yet this chapter on Kierkegaard's reflections on immortality and its positive expression—blessedness—

---

*Ludwig Feuerbach, *Das Wesen des Christenthums* (Leipzig, 1841). More about the relations between race and the individual, and about immortality, especially in the chapters: *"Der Unterschied des Christenthums vom Heidenthum"* and *"Der christliche Himmel oder die persönliche Unsterblichkeit."*

would be incomplete if mention were not made of the fact that one also meets unexpectedly other tones in Kierkegaard. We find a certain reservation about the extreme consequences, as in this statement: "Nevertheless it always seems to me that in spite of the profound nonsense in which we are stuck fast we shall all, however, be saved."[146]

Kierkegaard could say the same thing still more emphatically by bringing himself into the question. We read (probably from the end of 1854):

> But I do not pretend to be better than others. What the old Bishop said about me—that I talked as if everybody else was on the road to hell—is simply not true. No, if anyone wants to be able to say that I talk about going to hell, then I talk like this—"If the rest are all going to hell, then I am going along." This is the way I speak if anyone is able to say in any sense that I talk about going to hell. But I do not believe it. On the contrary, I believe that we will all be saved—and I, too—something which arouses my deepest wonder.*

These more or less contradictory reflections on the problem of immortality come from Kierkegaard's latest *Journals*. During the conflict with the church itself, he was forced by the very nature of the affair to emphasize more consistently in an ironical way the existential aspect.**

A survey of Søren Kierkegaard's reflections on immortality shows that a tension must inevitably come between the dogmatic starting point which says that all men have the Eternal within themselves and the existential approach which says that man does not become immortal, does not become a self, except by

---

*This note may be considered as a parallel to the statement by Climacus that "a truly religious man" will doubt most of all his own salvation (*Pap.* XI³ B 57, p. 105. See also *S.V.* VII, p. 337, first note; *Concluding Unscientific Postscript,* p. 348).

**An example of this may be found in "The Instant, No. 2," in the section entitled "The Comfortable and—the Concern for Eternal Salvation" (*S.V.* XIV, p. 122; *Attack Upon Christendom,* p. 99).

an existential transformation through a true relationship to the Eternal. Even if Kierkegaard as an edifying author could evade this problem, he could not as a thinker avoid seeing the difficulties. The very fact that he so strongly emphasizes the existential side of human existence makes immortality and the self seem completely dependent on a transformation of existence.

Kierkegaard has not given us a contradiction-free solution of "one of the most difficult" problems. Perhaps it cannot and will not be solved intellectually. Kierkegaard lets both lines of thought stand side by side. They belong together as a condition and in the fulfillment of this condition they belong together. However, Kierkegaard's great service is that he is not satisfied with a dim conception of the problem of the individual, race, and immortality, but points out the difficulties of the problem and tries to illuminate them deeply and from all sides through rigorous thinking.

# VI. *The Dialectic of Freedom*

In a Journal entry in 1845 Kierkegaard says, "Perhaps what we need most now to throw a light on the relationship between logic and ontology is a study of the concepts of possibility, actuality, and necessity."[147] Although Kierkegaard in this note calls for an examination of possibility, actuality, and necessity, he himself had and employed a quite definite understanding of these concepts and their relation to each other. It is the purpose of this chapter to show that behind his divergent and apparently contradictory reflections lies a thoughtful, integrated conception, a conception worthy of closer acquaintance and capable of forming the basis for a more extensive inquiry into the issue.

Kierkegaard himself indicates the relationship between the three concepts in the formulation: "actuality is a unity of possibility and necessity."[148] With this formulation as a starting point, we shall try to show how Kierkegaard applies it to the different forms of actuality. In developing the concept of actuality we shall simultaneously designate the different stages in the progress of freedom. The essential question, after all, is freedom, the "dialectical in the determinants of possibility and necessity."[149] In the end it will be apparent why a study of the problem of freedom lends itself in a particular way to "illuminating the relationship between the logical and the ontological." In order that the study may not give the impression of a dialectic remote from actuality, we shall often use concrete examples as illustrations. Moreover, we shall proceed in this study from the lower forms of actuality in the direction of the actuality of spirit.

We begin with the actuality of nature. As a simple example of this actuality we may use a star[150] to see what is meant by the fact that as actuality it is a synthesis of possibility and necessity. When we look at a star as an immediate actuality, we can regard it from two points of view: according to the determinant of being or according to the determinant of essence. From the point of view of being we see that something exists, and from the point of view of essence we see what it is that exists. Everything will always be regarded from these two points of view. The essence of a thing corresponds to its concept or necessity, while its being depends upon its possibility, i.e., the actualized possibility. A star, when it is seen, is a unity of the determinants of being and essence and thereby a unity of the actualized possibility and essence. The very moment one thinks about this star there is a change in its being but not in its essence. Being as actuality cannot be thought. Every time we try to think it, we change it to possibility. It is different with the determinant essence. Whether one sees a star or thinks about it, the concept of star is not changed. Necessity remains unchanged. The star as a thought actuality is thus a unity of possibility and necessity. The star as immediate actuality is a unity of actualized possibility and necessity. Consequently, the change occurs only in the sphere of being and not in the sphere of essence.*

From the physical world as actuality and necessity we go to organic nature. The physical world is the condition and the possibility for this next and higher actuality.** In organic nature we see a development in that living organisms apparently by themselves accomplish the transition from possibility to actuality and thereby actualize the elements of their essence. Kierkegaard limits this transition, however, to an absolute obedience to the Creator, as we see in the following quotation: "In nature everything is unconditional obedience; here it is not merely that nothing happens without his will, nothing whatsoever—as is the case in the human world because God is almighty—no, here there is more, for everything is absolute obedience."[151]

With man a new element appears. All of organic nature, with the exception of man, is completely bound to finite ends. Only for man is it true that his end is the Eternal. Therefore the formulation that actuality is a synthesis of possibility and necessity acquires a new meaning for human actuality. By obeying the Creator, man is also on the way to the Eternal; thus the transition to the true actuality, which is the reality of the Eternal,

---

*Here, already, comes the question about the first cause of this transition from possibility to actuality. Kierkegaard's answer takes it for granted that everything which comes into existence "points back ultimately to a freely effecting cause" (*S.V.* IV, p. 239). Every honest scholar will at least hold open this question about the first movement. Only the materialistic theories are quick to settle the question by explaining everything without any transcendence. But their explanations are built upon the most amazing supposition to date—namely this, that irrational material components all by themselves, by necessity or by accident, have in the course of time produced something as rational as a dialectical materialist.

**Kierkegaard apparently starts from the Aristotelian tradition in his development of the concept.

is assured. It is interesting that Kierkegaard has conceived of this as being man's original state, even though there seems to be only one place where he describes it.[152] But in *The Concept of Dread* he also bases his reflections on original sin on the presupposition of this original state. It is the temptation to eat of the tree of knowledge which drives man to disobedience. Knowledge in the form of reflection breaks down the primitive state of innocence, and history begins. If man looks more closely at the newness which reflection brings, he is torn away from his basic repose in the present, and past and future appear. Furthermore, a change occurs in that man, with the help of reflection, can set a goal for his striving and his actions. Man will himself shape the new actuality. This actuality may again be regarded within the formulation: the unity of possibility and necessity. A few examples may throw a light here. A man wishes to achieve something definite in this world. A gulf opens between the present actuality and the future actualization. The actuality which is to be achieved is first of all something definite and consequently as essence comes under necessity; simultaneously this actualization as something possible only in the future may be considered as coming under possibility. When the new actualization is achieved, it occurs again only by the transformation in the sphere of being from possibility to actuality. Essence cannot be changed since that would mean giving up the goal.

We may use a more simple example. An architect draws a plan for a house he intends to build. The design for the house, which is to be a new actuality, is necessary because it is a definite and particular house which is going to be built, and it is possible because the house is capable of being constructed. When the house is built, the necessity is unchanged since it is this particular house which has been built.* Moreover, there has been no change in the essence. The change concerns only being and signifies that this thing which was only possible now has become actual. It is apparent that the future actuality always embraces possibility and necessity as the two elements of the synthesis. The change occurs only in being. By such external actions man shapes historical actuality.

As an outcome of this view of the historical, Kierkegaard came into opposition with Hegel's conception. As already indicated, Kierkegaard regarded it an error to see existence from the side of only one of the elements. The error is compounded when Hegel finally permits actualized possibility to become changed to necessity. From Kierkegaard's point of view existence must always be considered simultaneously under the two qualifications—being and essence. We may, of course, concentrate our attention upon one of the elements of the compound, but we must not forget the other element. Kierkegaard also shows that the fact that each of the two elements may be particularly emphasized leads to two principal points of view by which existence can be interpreted—namely, the philosophical and the historical. If one is interested in the concept and the essence of things, he is led to philosophy. If, on the other hand, one is interested in origins and factual being, he comes to history. But philosophy cannot do without a relation to the actual any more than history can do without the conceptual. For essence (philosophy) without being (the link to actuality) is a phantom or an unreal fantasy, and being without essence is nothing. Nor can one element become the other—as Hegel maintained

---

*Compare *Pap.* V B 15, 1: "If, for example, my plan is changed in coming into existence, then it is no longer my plan but another plan, which has come into existence. However, if it comes into existence unchanged, then it is my plan. Herein lies the unchanged. But coming into existence is also a change. This change is from non-being to being.

about actuality, which became necessity by apprehension. That which has movement for its presupposition can never fall under the heading of necessity alone. When a design is carried out or a goal is reached, this historical fact is still a synthesis of the two elements, and every time I think it historically both elements are represented.*

Since, in the transition from possibility to actuality, necessity remains unchanged, necessity is the common invariable factor in the synthesis before and after the transition. Kierkegaard could therefore allow in his outline for *Philosophical Fragments* a formulation which sounds quite Hegelian: "Necessity is the union of possibility and actuality."[153] If we regard the synthesis at its transition as possibility/necessity becoming in transition actuality/necessity, we discern that the formulation of the synthesis above is supportable. When Kierkegaard nevertheless rejected this formulation, it was not only to avoid confusion with Hegel's concept but also to emphasize that his own principal concern was with the existential and not with the conceptual. Nor has he left us any special study of the concept of necessity; on the contrary, we have extensive treatments of the concepts of possibility and actuality.**

Until now we have been concerned with movement or freedom in man whose goal lies within the finite world. That which is called "world history" has only a visible and finite goal, and the framework of its unfolding may be the race, the folk, or

---

*In my opinion Dr. Johannes Sløk in his book *Forsynstanken* has discerned most penetratingly the problem of freedom in Kierkegaard, and at the same time he has taken his position with regard to Kierkegaard's attack on Hegel's concept of history. But Sløk's solution is unsatisfactory in that his concept of freedom (influenced, perhaps by Bergson) falls short, in the end, of a relationship to necessity.

**Even if someone were able to prove that Kierkegaard only wanted to jot down the Hegelian concept in his outline, this still would not change the points I have made, for they are supported by Kierkegaard's own structuring of the synthesis and not by different wordings of it.

the state. The movement of freedom, which has only a finite goal, is itself finite and relative and consequently is also an actuality which is attained here—a relative actuality. In this finite, relative actuality, subjectivity corresponds with objectivity and inwardness resembles outwardness. A project or a striving which is only a subjective wish may be realized as something outward. Here the quantitative dialectic is everywhere relevant, since reason and history can control finitude. A man's achievements may be quantitatively evaluated and attractively inserted in history books, which means that access to world history is through the quantitative dialectic, and anything which has become world history has gone through this dialectic.[154] Kierkegaard characterizes this relative actuality by the expression "the possibility of the possible,"[155] which signifies that the historical generally is a possibility for the next stage—the possibility of the Eternal.

The freedom which has concerned us until now shows itself to be finite and limited, but a finite freedom is not freedom in the truest sense of the word, for "freedom is infinite and springs from nothing."[156] This sentence from *The Concept of Anxiety* creatively describes the new freedom which comes after the relative freedom and also describes the condition from which it emerges. This condition is expressed in the words "springs from nothing," which means that before there can be infinite freedom there must be a negation of relative goals and, along with it, of relative freedom. How radical this negation will be depends on how concrete the infinite is which appears to a man and demands this negation. Consequently there are levels in this negation of the finite to make room for the possibility, and later the actuality, of the Eternal.

To express the break with the finite Kierkegaard uses, for the most part, these three expressions: irony, resignation, and repentance. This trio also indicates the maximizing of the negation. Each of these negative qualifications must be taken as totalities, since they conclude a complete unity—namely, finiteness. Consequently, by irony we do not mean a degree of irony but an irony which permits all of the external world to perish, etc.

By negating the finite world as totality one comes to absolute freedom—but still only as a negative quality. But this negation is the condition necessary for the new positiveness, the freedom of the Eternal, to appear. The task now is to see how this new actuality relates itself to the actuality which has been negated.

We consider first of all irony and that possibility of the infinite which has irony as its premise. Irony, through understanding, negates the ultimate validity of social and moral laws which attain their highest expression in the life of the folk and the state. Irony lays the foundation for a new orientation by leveling all values having a this-worldly end. Consequently the very actuality of folk and state comes under the judgment of irony. After its negation, finite actuality, as a synthesis of possibility and necessity, will be subordinated to the new actuality, which again must be scrutinized under the determinants being and essence. Kierkegaard presents Socrates as the historical example of this attempt to form the synthesis "finitude-infinitude" subsequent to his having created the condition for such a synthesis through irony.

Considered from the standpoint of being and essence, the synthesis looks like this: possibility and necessity as determinants of the finite must be subordinated to possibility and necessity as determinants of the infinite. The task in existence becomes that of forming a unity out of this reduplication. In *The Sickness unto Death,* where this stage in man's synthesis is also described, Kierkegaard states it simply by saying that man is a synthesis of possibility and necessity. He omits possibility in the first part of the reduplication and necessity in the second part, so that the formulation has the appearance of being used on a lower level of actuality and not for a reduplication. One who knows Kierkegaard's concious intention to make a matter more difficult precisely by means of simplification will find this quite in order. But Kierkegaard also had a good reason for this simplification. It will be apparent later that it is in the lower stage of actuality that necessity is more significant, in the higher stage it is possibility (freedom). By this principle, then, the reduplication, and therefore *finitude-infinitude,* can be expressed only by the more decisive element of each level of the reduplication.

We must turn once more to Socrates to see what happens and how it happens when Socrates tries to introduce the Eternal into existence. Socrates has attained the essence of the Eternal, its necessity and possibility, by *recollection.*[157] From this abstract Eternal he comes by the risk of faith to the absolutely concrete: that he also is eternal (immortal) and—it is one and the same— that there is a personal God.[158] This he will now express in his existence. He will act in such a manner that he stands more in dread of this invisible power than of the visible powers. Socrates tries to find an expression for this belief in a world of relativities, and his attempt goes in the direction of a synthesis of finitude and infinitude. But can the Eternal find a concrete expression in that which is finite? To answer this question we must once more scrutinize the commensurability which existed between the internal and the external in "world history." There a plan or an endeavor as inward possibility could find its external expression. The plan or wish aimed at something finite and could be visibly realized in the external. But the Eternal cannot be represented this way by finite modes of expression. If one tries to do this, he "finitizes" the infinite. That which is infinite can never be merged with a visible effect, since a visible effect is something finite. The essence of the Eternal is that it is Eternal, and it can never be exhausted in relative relationships. Consequently one can never render the Eternal by means of the visible or by anything which can become an object for us. Only for the subject is it possible to affirm the Eternal by bestowing an absolute meaning upon a definite action. The Eternal can be denoted only by the subject's infinite concern and not by any objective means. Previously subjectivity could be completely merged with objectivity; now something incommensurate arises between the external expression of an act and the interpenetrating subjective meaning. For this reason two apparently identical actions can lie in two qualitatively different spheres, and it is the subject's concern with the infinite which determines the rank of the two actions. In "world history" it is action which proclaims itself; the more exceptional and grandiose it is, the more significant it is. Now, on the contrary, "neither the qualitative *how* nor the quantitative *what* determines the significance."[159] Thought cannot grasp the new actuality which results from this synthesis. Thought can grasp the objectivity of an action, but it cannot grasp the fact that under this objectivity something infinite could be hiding. It regards such a contradictory reality as a paradox. For this reason Socrates, with his existential probing, is on the path of the paradox. For this reason, too, his path became, in Kierkegaard's eyes, definitely analagous to the paradox of faith, even though this lies on a higher plane.

In contrast to irony, resignation indicates a deeper negative movement away from finitude. Irony (and particularly humor) presupposes the Eternal in man. In resignation man collides with the transcendent. In irony and humor there is still a last frontier, the Eternal in man, which forms the dividing line between human actuality and the transcendent. In resignation the complete negation is accomplished. It is the Eternal as transcendent which requires the movement of resignation as a condition for the possibility of dialogue between the Eternal and man. This resignation, analogous to irony, becomes the condition for a new synthesis. Perhaps it is unnecessary to point out that there is a difference of degree between Abraham's resignation and the resignation of the Middle Ages, but common to both is the fact that the transcendent has become evident to men, even though it is more or less abstractly conceived. At this stage, the synthesis is to a more essential degree stamped by the paradox which was mentioned before in connection with the freedom which presupposed irony.

Repentance as a totality is the highest negative expression of the break with existence.* Through it man moves into relationship with the concrete transcendence which is revealed truth. After irony and resignation, man still does not have true knowledge of himself, of his bondage to relative goals, but his attempt to form the synthesis between the claims of the infinite and the life in time reveals man's bankruptcy. Through his seeking, man becomes matured enough to receive the truth about himself—that he loves perishable things more than he loves God. Only now, only by the movement of repentance can man come to absolute freedom, to God. Kierkegaard characterizes this movement in the following ways: "I repent myself out of all existence,"[160] or, "He repents himself back into himself, back into the family, back into the race, until he finds himself in God."[161]

---

*See *S.V.* VI, pp. 442 ff.; *Stages on Life's Way*, p. 430: "A man's highest inward act is to repent. But to repent is not a positive movement outward or in the direction of something, but a negative movement inward; not *a doing* but a letting something *be done* to oneself."

Seeking further to form a new synthesis (after the movement of repentance) by relating himself absolutely to the
absolute and relatively to the relative, a man is led to a more
stringent definition of total guilt and sin. Since Kierkegaard
has described this process so extensively and completely in
*Concluding Unscientific Postscript,* it is not necessary to go
further into the matter, except to emphasize the aspects which
pertain to the problem of freedom and the new actuality.

It has been shown that as long as the movement of freedom
is within the world of relativity it can attain its goal. Furthermore, a man is able to act justly when it is a matter of "the
ethical in the sense of morality"* or of civic morality. In other
words, one can manage to be a good citizen in this world. It is
not until he is a citizen of the eternal world that one discovers
his bondage, and this he discovers to the same degree that the
requirement to act according to his eternal meaning is sharpened within him. By seeking to fulfill this requirement, one is
on the way from the infinite as possibility to the infinite as
actuality, and this actuality reveals to man that he is a sinner
in need of forgiveness. This last actuality is an absolute paradox. It is contrary to human understanding that a man can
become absolutely guilty. It is also contrary to human understanding that this absolute guilt can be forgiven.[162] Only for
faith is the paradox true actuality, and "the passion of faith is
the only thing which overcomes the absurdity."[163]

How this paradoxical actuality makes a joke of all quantitative calculations may easily be illustrated by an example from
quite another situation. In the common-sense world in which
we live a sum of money means what the amount says, and a
good deed can be reckoned by the amount of the contribution.

*Kierkegaard uses three meanings for ethical in his writings. Together they
encompass the whole domain of ethics.

It is altogether different when a man comes under the eternal demand: thou shalt be merciful. Then the external *what* is completely disregarded and only the *how* is important. One who is able to give nothing gives equally as much when he is merciful as one who gives a great sum out of mercy. The qualification mercy is established by the Eternal and "to reckon with an infinite amount is impossible, for to reckon is simply to render something finite."[164] For this reason deeds of mercy can never come under ordinary human calculations.

One who lives under the paradox always comes to live in a "duality."* As long as this life in paradox is in the world, it can by virtue of its external data be properly placed under the heading "world history," but its subjective side becomes a hidden life which only exists for itself and cannot become an object of observation.

If, from this last position, we look at the way in which the relationship between being and existence (and in our special case between possibility and necessity), as the elements of the synthesis, develops, a clear and definite interrelation between these elements clearly emerges. Kierkegaard tries to describe this dependence by a simple sketch[165] (he uses it in expanded form in his works) where the relationship between freedom and necessity can also be seen. According to this sketch one could construct a graduated instrument on which would be registered at the lowest degree everything wholly qualified by essence and necessity. Being, on the other hand, would be only hypothetical. This "thermometer" would rise to the same de-

---

*Kierkegaard says, "If . . . the Eternal is in a man the Eternal duplicates itself in him in such a way that every moment it is in him it is in him in a double mode: in an outward direction and in an inward direction back into itself —but in such a way that it is one and the same—otherwise it would not be a reduplication" (*S.V.* II, p. 159, IX, p. 267; *Either/Or* II, p. 248; *Works of Love* p. 261).

gree that being together with freedom is accentuated. It is easy to see that the principle of subjectivity is the basis for the sketch. The more subjectivity, the more actuality.

Applied to the totality of our knowledge, this would mean that logic and mathematics would stand at the bottom of the column, for even if their essence (necessity) is absolute, their being is only hypothetical. The next degree, which would encompass nature, belongs mostly under necessity, but here being is already much more accentuated than in the completely abstract sciences.

Where man is concerned, being has decisive significance, and this fact changes the meaning of existence. The line of development on the side of being (freedom) could look something like this in man: first, "possibility of the possible," corresponding to historical actuality, then "possibility" as the first reflection of the Eternal, and after that the actuality of the Eternal itself. On the side of essence there would first be necessity in nature, then the whole of finitude as necessity, and then, to the same degree in which freedom is accentuated, necessity would show itself as man's bondage to the relative and would come under the rubric of guilt.[166] Every time a man seeks to actualize the possibility of the Eternal, and the higher the degree of his searching, the more he discovers that his essence is guilt. The concrete actuality which is Christ at last helps man to the insight that his essence is not some indifferent necessity which might still be considered to be low on the scale—but sin. It is freedom which, by transition from the one possibility to the next actuality, and at last by the leap into the absolute actuality, makes man into a sinner. Without the movement of freedom, there is no sin. Only as a sinner can a man come to stand in the right relationship to the last and only actuality, to the God of revelation.

Only of God's being can it be said that he, as absolute subjectivity and freedom, completely determines his own essence.
Consequently it would be incorrect to use the word necessity,
as some thinkers do, in relation to God's essence. God's essence
is the Good itself in its unchangeableness. Kierkegaard points
out that God's unchangeableness is closely knit to God's absolute freedom and subjectivity, as can be seen in these selected
quotations: "In unchanged clarity he, the Father of light, is
eternally unchanged. In unchanged clarity—yes, precisely for
this reason he is unchanged, for he is pure clarity, a clarity
in which there is no darkness and which no darkness can
approach."[167] "God is the pure subjectivity—perfect, pure subjectivity. There is no external being in him, none whatsoever.
Everything that has any such objectivity enters thereby into
the realm of relativity."[168]

In the quotation used to introduce this chapter, Kierkegaard
anticipates that the study of possibility, actuality, and necessity
would also illuminate the relationship "between logic and
ontology." If it is clear by now that Kierkegaard conceals two
areas—ultimately metaphysics and dogmatics—in these apparently innocent pairs of concepts which we meet in certain portions of his works, then one sees that the quotation just mentioned expresses the conviction that a study of the problem of
freedom should help us to settle the boundary dispute between
knowledge and faith. By following the path which freedom
takes, it should be possible to find a place where one could say
that here reason stops and it is no longer possible to travel the
path of logic.

Kierkegaard pinpoints just such a place when he says, "Any
definition in which being is the primary determinant lies outside the immanental thought and therefore outside of logic."[169]
Accordingly, the dividing line "between logic and ontology"

lies at the point where the Eternal as an existential determinant breaks through. Not until this has happened may we say that it is being which is the primary determinant. Logic has to surrender at this dividing line. Logical thought cannot grasp the new actuality which emerges with the synthesis—finitude-infinitude—since this actuality stands under the sign of the absurd.

Logic can discern only finitude and finite determinants. Speculation, therefore, may interest itself in historical actuality insofar as it belongs to finitude. For even if it is possible to say that all change is a paradox and therefore impervious to thought, nevertheless change within the finite is only relatively paradoxical, and relative paradoxes can be mediated. But the speculation which can "digest"[170] this relative, paradoxical actuality reaches its boundary at the absolute paradoxical reality.

Logic, then, as quantitative dialectic, can embrace the finite and be the foundation for the various sciences, but it has to surrender to the qualitative dialectic of the reality which appears when the Eternal enters into existence. In Volume VII A 84 of the *Journals* Kierkegaard writes: "Everything depends on making the distinction between the quantitative and the qualitative dialectics absolute. All of logic is a quantitative dialectic or a modal dialect, for everything is, and the whole is one and the same. The qualitative dialectic belongs to existence." (By "existence" Kierkegaard here means actuality penetrated by the Eternal.)

On one side we have actuality penetrated by our understanding and on the other side the actuality of absurdity. "The absurd comes to an end negatively before the sphere of faith, which is a sphere *sui generis*."[171] The qualitative dialectic teaches us to respect the absolute distinction between the two spheres— knowledge and faith. It is freedom's dialectical development which can throw a light on the separation between the areas of dogmatics and metaphysics.

The dialectic of freedom outlined here is but a single link in Kierkegaard's consistently worked out concept of the categories of existence in their dialectical wholeness. Until this wholeness-view is worked through and understood, it is completely hopeless to begin a critical evaluation of Kierkegaard's thought. As has already happened, a critique of separate points in Kierkegaard's dialectical thought-structure would only result in this: Supposing one's analysis to be a critique of Kierkegaard's ideas, one merely assaults his own misinterpretations of Kierkegaard's thought.

# VII. *The Dialectic of Communication*

Kierkegaard realized early in his authorship that next in importance to knowing the truth is knowing how to communicate it to others. In his theory of the stages he had an over-view of all the possible postures of man, but in order to apply this knowledge effectively he had to look for a corresponding theory of the art of communication. He therefore worked out an original theory of communication and used it consistently in his authorship. It is possible here to touch upon only a few of the principles in this comprehensive and fundamental dialectic of communication.*

---

*Information about Kierkegaard's dialectic of communication can be found scattered throughout his works and journals. The most extensive and detailed treatment of this subject is found in the "Dialectic of Communication" in *Journals,* VIII² B 79-89, which is a preparatory work to a series of lectures which Kierkegaard never delivered. The same subject is treated also in *Collected Works,* VII, pp. 55 ff.; XIII, pp. 529 ff.; and XII, pp. 115 ff.; *Concluding Unscientific Postscript,* pp. 67 ff.; *The Point of View,* pp. 22 ff. and *Training in Christianity,* pp. 122 ff. The art of communication also includes Kierkegaard's literary style, but this is not discussed here because Professor F. J. Billeskov Jansen has recently written a knowledgeable book about this subject under the title: *Studier i Søren Kierkegaards litterære Kunst.*

Kierkegaard found in Socrates one of the significant principles of how to communicate the truth. Socrates in his day had a communication problem similar to that of Kierkegaard, only at a lower level. He wished to draw man's attention to the Eternal in his own inner self. Kierkegaard wished to call attention to the revelation of the Eternal in time (Christ). Socrates carried out his task by placing himself in the other man's position and leading him on from that point. Kierkegaard also, as can be seen in his book *The Point of View for My Work as an Author,* started with this Socratic rule. Kierkegaard wrote: "To succeed in truth to bring a man to a certain place one must first and foremost be sure to find him where *he* is and begin there."[172] Socrates solved his problem by using the dialogue to enter into different men's thinking in order to help them. Kierkegaard's task was to achieve the same thing in his writing. He tried to reach men by presenting the many different conditions of life so that a man might find somewhere in his works his own existential position, and then, from there, move toward the truth.

Kierkegaard used both pseudonyms and his own name in writing about the different conditions of life. Relevant to this, it may be noted that the ingenious Kierkegaard "travels through and experiences the whole past" in the history of man as if every possibility were his own—until "he catches up with himself"[173] in the religious stage. In the beginning of his authorship the possibility of the aesthetic and human-ethical stages were past for him, and he had to begin with the ethical-religious position. He used pseudonyms in writing about those positions which he had passed beyond. He set his own name to the position in which he himself was personally involved. Later he used still two more pseudonyms—H. H. is the pseudonymous author of *Two Minor Ethico-Religious Treatises* and Anti-Climacus is the pseudonymous author of *The Sickness unto Death* and

*Training in Christianity.* The last two books, however, had
Kierkegaard's name as publisher.

These last two pseudonyms express that Kierkegaard dared
to go farther—positively as well as negatively—than his own
existential experience. In this way he has neither passed himself off to be an apostle or a martyr (the extreme possibility in
*Two Minor Ethico-Religious Treatises* and in *Training in Christianity*) nor has he denied the truth of Christianity (the extreme
possibility in *The Sickness unto Death*). Thus we get two kinds
of pseudonyms—those writing from a lower level than Kierkegaard's own existential religious position and those writing
from a higher level, pointing farther. His own position lies
somewhere between, or as he himself expresses it in a short
statement: "I have characterized myself higher than Joh.
Climacus and lower than Anti-Climacus."[174] We must remember, however, that Joh. Climacus is to Kierkegaard the highest
and most comprehensive pseudonym of all the lower-position
pseudonyms, since Joh. Climacus analyzes them all critically
from his position in *Concluding Unscientific Postscript.*

In addition to mapping the way of Christian development,
Kierkegaard, by means of his pseudonyms, furnishes us with
no end of possible positions below the Christian. The whole
structure of his writing thus becomes a branching tree-system
representing all the possibilities of human existence. Relevant
to this Kierkegaard says: "I hope to achieve this by my writings:
to leave behind such an accurate description of what it is to be
a Christian and a Christian's relationships in the world that a
noble and zealous youth may find it as accurate a map of relationships as any topographic map he may obtain from the cele-
brated institutes. I myself have not had such assistance from any
author. The teachers of the ancient church left out one side. They
did not know the world."[175] These life-positions are described

so consistently and sharply that they are easily recognized. Kierkegaard achieves this result by letting the pseudonyms "pursue a one-sided course to the very extreme."[176] In this way he achieves a unique result. In his writing he is able to find man wherever he is, right or wrong, and is able to speak to all, regardless of their spiritual condition. This, then, is his redeeming (maieutic) art, which he also, using Socrates' expression, calls the art of communication.

This art of communication leads most often to indirect communication. The pseudonymous works are indirect in every instance. Kierkegaard regards the edifying literature as direct communication, but we must not forget that even here he does not lay himself bare. He communicates only what is necessary to give an accurate description of the religious way.

Kierkegaard's method of posing opposites is also related to indirect communication. His intention is to hasten the individual to making a choice. We find the best example of this method in the work which began his authorship, *Either-Or,* where two opposite courses are placed side by side and it is left to the individual to make his choice. An example of the same method at a higher level is found in *Training in Christianity.* In this serious work humor is used in those places where earnestness is to be emphasized. The appearance of Christ in Copenhagen is described humorously, and yet there is a terrible earnestness and condemnation in the fact that Christ, everywhere and in any age, would be treated by the world in the very same manner. One may laugh when he reads the sketch in *Training in Christianity,* but he ought rather to weep over the way in which truth is received. This method leaves it completely up to the reader whether he will laugh or cry. In this manner the indirect method allows the individual's own thought to come forward.

Another device in Kierkegaard's art of communication is his

deliberate way of occasionally making his writing difficult to read. He speaks about this with a certain glee. His aim was to prevent hasty parroting of his thoughts. He knew, too, the value of writing which takes effort to penetrate.* The tendency of the age was to get hasty results. By creating difficulties Kierkegaard wished to hinder a skimming through pages which had been written with his heart's blood. He did his very best to awaken the individual to independent thought and activity.

Kierkegaard's authorship was in the service of Christianity. Using his "eminent talents," he erected a defense against all superficial attacks on Christianity, well aware that "the Eternal is still the most powerful in intellectual disputes."[177] He was able to "bind those knots again which superficial thinking has so long tried to undo."[178] With triumphant joy he says, "The battle which I have won consists in successfully establishing category-relationships in respect to what it is to be a Christian so firmly that no dialecticians will be able to undo them. I have rightly seen that that which will again stand fast is not Christianity but the fact of being a Christian; after this I place the concept of contemporaneity, and then the possibility of offense, and finally, the concept of faith as the first and highest of all concepts."[179] Kierkegaard anticipated that Christianity would once again have power over the minds of men and be the central point in human existence only after terrible conflicts in the future. With his authorship he has created for this battle to come "a completely new military science."[180]

A quotation from Kierkegaard in which he lets a future poet

*For one of several examples see *Collected Works,* VII, p. 255; *Concluding Unscientific Postscript,* pp. 264-5: "So it is left to the reader himself to piece things together by his own endeavors, if he so desires, but nothing is done for the reader's indolence." See also *Journals,* VIII² B. 88, pp. 184 ff.: "The task must be made difficult—for only the difficult inspires the high-minded. . . ." It is quite understandable, then, why Kierkegaard would not give an easy survey-exposition of the theory of the stages.

hold forth on Kierkegaard provides a good conclusion to this study:

He served the cause of Christianity; from childhood his life was oriented toward this in a wonderful way. He fulfilled the task of reflection—to place Christianity, that is, what it is to become a Christian, wholly and adequately into reflection. The purity of his heart was to will only one thing. The very thing which his contemporaries condemned him for while he lived—that he did not reduce the requirement or give in—this very same thing will be praised by later generations—that he did not reduce the requirement or give in. But the huge undertaking did not deceive him; while dialectically, as author, he had a vision of the whole, as a Christian he understood that the whole thing meant for him personally to be trained in Christianity. He could not dedicate his dialectic structure, parts of which already are independent works, to any man, still less to himself. If to anyone, it had to be to the Governing Power, to whom, in fact, the author had daily and yearly dedicated it—the author, who historically died from a mortal disease but poetically died of longing for the Eternal, of longing to do nothing else but give unceasing thanks to God.[181]

# Bibliography and Notes

The works used for quotation and reference are

*Søren Kierkegaards Samlede Vaerker* [*Collected Works*], edited by A. B. Drachmann, J. L. Heiberg, and H. O. Lange. Published in Copenhagen by Gyldendal, 1901. Reference to the original Danish is by the abbreviation: *S.V. Søren Kierkegaards Papirer* [*Journals*], edited by P. A. Heiberg and Victor Kuhr. Published in Copenhagen by Gyldendal, 1909-1948. Reference to the original Danish is by the abbreviation: *Pap.*

Translations from the *Works* and the *Journals* are from the Danish, and the sources are indicated in the notes following. For those who accept the invitation of the *Introduction* to read the works themselves, the quotations from the *Works* are collated with these English translations listed below.

## Bibliography

*Attack upon Christendom.* Translated by Walter Lowrie. Princeton: Princeton University Press, 1946.

*Christian Discourses.* Translated by Walter Lowrie. London: Oxford University Press, 1939.

*The Concept of Dread* [*Angst:* Anxiety]. Translated by Walter Lowrie. Princeton: Princeton University Press, 1946.

*Concluding Unscientific Postscript to the "Philosophical Fragments."* Translated by David F. Swenson; completed and edited by Walter Lowrie. Princeton: Princeton University Press, 1944.

*Edifying Discourses.* I-IV. Translated by David F. and Lillian Marvin Swenson. Minneapolis: Augsburg Publishing House, 1943-45. (Now also available in 2 vols. issued by the same publisher in 1962.)

*Edifying Discourses, A Selection.* Translated by David F. and Lillian Marvin Swenson. Edited with an introduction by Paul L. Holmer. New York: Harper and Brothers, 1958.

*Either/Or: A Fragment of Life.* Volume I translated by David F. and Lillian Marvin Swenson; Volume II translated by Walter Lowrie. Princeton: Princeton University Press, 1944.

*Fear and Trembling.* Translated by Walter Lowrie. Princeton: Princeton University Press, 1941.

*For Self-Examination*. Translated by Edna and Howard Hong. Minneapolis: Augsburg Publishing House, 1940.

*The Gospel of Suffering*. Translated by David F. and Lillian Marvin Swenson. Minneapolis: Augsburg Publishing House, 1948.

*Philosophical Fragments*. Translated by David F. Swenson. Commentary by Niels Thulstrup. Translation revised and Commentary translated by Howard V. Hong. Princeton: Princeton University Press, 1962.

*The Point of View for My Work as an Author*. Translated by Walter Lowrie. London: Oxford University Press, 1939.

*Purity of Heart Is to Will One Thing*. Rev. ed. Translated by Douglas V. Steere. New York: Harper and Brothers, 1948.

*Repetition*. Translated by Walter Lowrie. Princeton: Princeton University Press, 1941.

*The Sickness unto Death*. Translated by Walter Lowrie. Princeton: Princeton University Press, 1941.

*Stages on Life's Way*. Translated by Walter Lowrie. Princeton: Princeton University Press, 1940.

*Training in Christianity*. Translated by Walter Lowrie. Princeton: Princeton University Press, 1944.

*Works of Love*. Translated by Edna and Howard Hong. New York: Harper and Brothers, 1962.

# Notes

(See above for explanation of abbreviations and arrangement.)

1. *Pap.*, IX B 64, p. 379.
2. *S.V.*, XIII, p. 605; *The Point of View for My Work as an Author*, p. 132.
3. *S.V.*, VII, p. 47; *Concluding Unscientific Postscript*, p. 59.
4. *Pap.*, XI$^3$ B 109, pp. 178 ff.
5. *Pap.*, I A 75, p. 53.
6. *Pap.*, VII A 127.
7. *S.V.*, IV, p. 313; *The Concept of Dread*, p. 37.
8. *S.V.*, IV, p. 313; *Ibid.*, p. 38.
9. *S.V.*, IV, p. 314; *Ibid.*, p. 39.
10. *S.V.*, IV, p. 313; *Ibid.*, p. 38.
11. *S.V.*, IV, p. 315; *Ibid.*, p. 40.
12. *S.V.*, VII, p. 375; *Concluding Unscientific Postscript*, p. 387.
13. *S.V.*, III, pp. 107 ff.; *Fear and Trembling*, pp. 84 ff.
14. *S.V.*, I, p. 44; *Either/Or*, I, p. 49.
15. *S.V.*, I, pp. 9, 10, 13, 15, 22 ff.; *Ibid.*, pp. 19, 20, 23, 24, 30 ff.
16. *S.V.*, IV, p. 341; *The Concept of Dread*, p. 65.
17. *Pap.*, V B 53, 27, p. 117. *S.V.*, IV, p. 338; *Ibid.*, p. 61.
18. *S.V.*, IV, p. 319; *Ibid.*, p. 44.
19. *S.V.*, I, p. 74; *Either/Or*, I, p. 75.
20. *S.V.*, I, p. 47; *Ibid.*, p. 51.

21. *S.V.*, I, p. 173; *Ibid.*, pp. 161-2.
22. *S.V.*, I, p. 203; *Ibid.*, p. 188.
23. *S.V.*, I, p. 248; *Ibid.*, p. 226.
24. *S.V.*, I, p. 227; *Ibid.*, p. 208.
25. *S.V.*, I, p. 267; *Ibid.*, p. 242.
26. *S.V.*, I, p. 268; *Ibid.*, p. 243.
27. *Pap.*, V B 53, 26.
28. *S.V.*, II, p. 165; *Either/Or*, II, p. 154.
29. *S.V.*, II, p. 166; *Ibid.*, p. 155.
30. *S.V.*, II, p. 170; *Ibid.*, p. 159.
31. *S.V.*, II, p. 172; *Ibid.*, p. 161.
32. *S.V.*, VII, p. 255; *Concluding Unscientific Postscript*, p. 264.
33. *S.V.*, VI, p. 45; *Stages on Life's Way*, p. 56.
34. *S.V.*, VI, p. 47; *Ibid.*, p. 59.
35. *S.V.*, VI, p. 49; *Ibid.*, p. 61.
36. *S.V.*, VI, p. 50; *Ibid.*, p. 62.
37. *S.V.*, VI, pp. 59 ff.; *Ibid.*, p. 70.
38. *S.V.*, VI, pp. 68 ff.; *Ibid.*, p. 79.
39. *S.V.*, VI, p. 70; *Ibid.*, p. 80.
40. *S.V.*, VI, p. 74; *Ibid.*, p. 84.
41. *S.V.*, VI, p. 76; *Ibid.*, p. 86.
42. *S.V.*, VI, p. 74; *Ibid.*, p. 84.
43. *S.V.*, VII, p. 255; *Concluding Unscientific Postscript*, p. 264.
44. *S.V.*, IV, p. 386; *The Concept of Dread*, p. 105.
45. *S.V.*, IV, p. 420; *Ibid.*, p. 137.
46. *S.V.*, III, p. 243; *Repetition*, p. 130.
47. *S.V.*, III, p. 84; *Fear and Trembling*, pp. 42-3.
48. *S.V.*, III, p. 146; *Ibid.*, p. 152.
49. *S.V.*, XIII, p. 336; *The Concept of Irony* (in translation).
50. *S.V.*, IV, p. 181; *Philosophical Fragments*, p. 14.
51. *S.V.*, VII, p. 191; *Concluding Unscientific Postscript*, p. 183.
52. *S.V.*, XI, p. 201; *The Sickness unto Death*, p. 145.
53. *S.V.*, II, p. 201; *Either/Or*, II, p. 188.
54. *S.V.*, II, p. 185; *Ibid.*, p. 173.
55. *S.V.*, II, p. 160; *Ibid.*, p. 149.
56. *S.V.*, II, p. 201; *Ibid.*, p. 189.
57. *S.V.*, II, p. 27; *Ibid.*, p. 25.
58. *S.V.*, II, pp. 59 ff.; *Ibid.*, pp. 54 ff.
59. *S.V.*, II, p. 80; *Ibid.*, p. 74.
60. *S.V.*, II, p. 96; *Ibid.*, p. 88.
61. *S.V.*, II, p. 223; *Ibid.*, p. 208.
62. *S.V.*, VI, p. 87; *Stages on Life's Way*, p. 97.
63. *S.V.*, VI, p. 114; *Ibid.*, p. 122.
64. *S.V.*, VI, p. 97; *Ibid.*, p. 106.
65. *S.V.*, VI, p. 98; *Ibid.*, p. 107.
66. *S.V.*, VI, p. 112; *Ibid.*, p. 120.
67. *S.V.*, VI, p. 135; *Ibid.*, p. 141.
68. *S.V.*, VI, p. 130; *Ibid.*, p. 137.
69. *S.V.*, VI, p. 130; *Ibid.*, p. 137.
70. *S.V.*, VI, p. 155; *Ibid.*, p. 160.
71. *S.V.*, VI, p. 162; *Ibid.*, p. 167.

72. *S.V.*, VI, p. 108; *Ibid.*, p. 116.
73. *S.V.*, VI, p. 161; *Ibid.*, p. 166.
74. *S.V.*, VI, p. 170; *Ibid.*, p. 174.
75. *S.V.*, VII, pp. 437 ff.; *Concluding Unscientific Postscript*, pp. 449 ff.
76. *S.V.*, VII, p. 498; *Ibid.*, p. 507.
77. *Pap.*, I A 89; I A 99, p. 70.
78. *Pap.*, II A 20; IX A 71.
79. *S.V.*, II, p. 270; *Either/Or*, II, p. 252.
80. *S.V.*, VI, pp. 189 ff., 219 ff., 236 ff., 259 ff., 302 ff., 336 ff.; *Stages on Life's Way*, pp. 191 ff., 220 ff., 236 ff., 258 ff., 302 ff., 330 ff.
81. *S.V.*, XIII, p. 565; *The Point of View*, p. 79.
82. *S.V.*, VI, p. 450; *Pap.* VIII A 649-650; *Stages on Life's Way*, pp. 435-6.
83. *Pap.*, II A 228.
84. *S.V.*, V, p. 168; *Edifying Discourses*, p. 143.
85. *S.V.*, VI, p. 414; *Stages on Life's Way*, p. 403.
86. *S.V.*, VIII, p. 144; *Purity of Heart*, p. 68.
87. *S.V.*, VIII, p. 178; *Ibid.*, p. 121.
88. *S.V.*, VIII, pp. 348-369; *The Gospel of Suffering*, pp. 65-96.
89. *Pap.*, X⁵ A 88, pp. 102 ff.
90. *Pap.*, X⁵ A 7.
91. *S.V.*, IX, p. 7; *Works of Love*, p. 17.
92. *S.V.*, IX, p. 115; *Ibid.*, p. 123.
93. *S.V.*, IX, p. 109; *Ibid.*, p. 117.
94. *S.V.*, IX, pp. 310 ff.; *Ibid.*, pp. 301-2.
95. *S.V.*, X, p. 181; *Christian Discourses*, p. 186.
96. *S.V.*, X, p. 232; *Ibid.*, p. 238.
97. *S.V.*, X, p. 211; *Ibid.*, p. 218.
98. *S.V.*, VII, pp. 488 ff.; *Concluding Unscientific Postscript*, pp. 496 ff.
99. *S.V.*, X, p. 238; *Christian Discourses*, p. 244.
100. *S.V.*, X, p. 241; *Ibid.*, p. 247.
101. *S.V.*, X, p. 240; *Ibid.*, p. 246.
102. *S.V.*, X, p. 316; *Ibid.*, p. 308.
103. *Pap.*, VIII¹ A 643.
104. *S.V.*, XII, p. 24; *Training in Christianity*, p. 28.
105. *S.V.*, XII, p. 48; *Ibid.*, p. 53.
106. *S.V.*, XII, p. 78; *Ibid.*, p. 83.
107. *S.V.*, XII, p. 95; *Ibid.*, p. 102.
108. *S.V.*, XII, p. 101; *Ibid.*, p. 108.
109. *S.V.*, XII, p. 100; *Ibid.*, p. 107.
110. *S.V.*, XII, p. 116; *Ibid.*, p. 123.
111. *S.V.*, XII, p. 125; *Ibid.*, p. 134.
112. *S.V.*, XII, p. 127; *Ibid.*, p. 136.
113. *S.V.*, XII, p. 232; *Ibid.*, p. 247.
114. *S.V.*, XI, p. 240; *The Sickness unto Death*, p. 216.
115. *S.V.*, XII, p. 267.
116. *S.V.*, XII, pp. 368 ff.; *For Self-Examination*, pp. 101-2.
117. *Pap.*, IV C 27.
118. *S.V.*, IV, p. 374; *The Concept of Dread*, p. 94.
119. *S.V.*, VII, p. 127; *Ibid.*, p. 138.
120. *S.V.*, VII, p. 146; *Concluding Unscientific Postscript*, p. 157.
121. *S.V.*, VII, p. 141; *Ibid.*, p. 152.

122. *S.V.*, VII, p. 144. See also *S.V.*, III, p. 195; *Ibid.*, p. 154. See also *Repetition*, pp. 44-5.
123. *S.V.*, VII, p. 146; *Concluding Unscientific Postscript*, p. 157.
124. *S.V.*, VII, pp. 146 ff.; *Ibid.*, pp. 157-8.
125. *S.V.*, VII, pp. 516 ff.; *Ibid.*, pp. 524 ff.
126. *Pap.*, VIII B 81, 8.
127. *S.V.*, XI, p. 127; *The Sickness unto Death*, p. 17.
128. *S.V.*, XI, pp. 191 ff.; *Ibid.*, pp. 126 ff.
129. *S.V.*, XI, pp. 192 ff.; *Ibid.*, p. 129.
130. *S.V.*, XI, pp. 223 ff.; *Ibid.*, p. 186.
131. *S.V.*, XI, pp. 212 and 229; *Ibid.*, pp. 165 and 197.
132. *S.V.*, V, pp. 81 ff; *Edifying Discourses*, Vol. IV, pp. 7-47.
133. *S.V.*, V, pp. 100 ff.; *Ibid.*, pp. 38 ff.
134. *S.V.*, X, pp. 203 ff.; *Christian Discourses*, pp. 210 ff.
135. *S.V.*, X, p. 213; *Ibid.*, p. 220.
136. *S.V.*, X, p. 204; *Ibid.*, p. 211.
137. *S.V.*, X, p. 207; *Ibid.*, p. 214.
138. *S.V.*, X, p. 206; *Ibid.*, p. 212.
139. *S.V.*, XIII, p. 567; *The Point of View*, p. 82.
140. *S.V.*, II, pp. 194 and 201; *Either/Or*, II, pp. 181-2, p. 194.
141. *S.V.*, III, p. 147; *Fear and Trembling*, p. 154.
142. *Pap.*, X⁴ A 440.
143. *Pap.*, XI² A 154.
144. *Pap.*, X¹ A 150. See also the quoted references to Plato, Aristotle, and Böhringer in the footnotes of the *Papirer*.
145. *Pap.*, XI¹ A 547.
146. *Pap.*, XI² A 244.
147. *Pap.*, VI B 54, 21.
148. *S.V.*, XI, p. 149; *The Sickness unto Death*, p. 55.
149. *S.V.*, XI, p. 142; *Ibid.*, p. 43.
150. *S.V.*, IV, p. 245; *Philosophical Fragments*, p. 100.
151. *S.V.*, XI, p. 28; *Christian Discourses*, p. 337.
152. *S.V.*, IV, pp. 24-25; *Edifying Discourses*, Vol. II, pp. 27-29.
153. *Pap.*, V B 15, 1.
154. *S.V.*, VII, p. 115; *Concluding Unscientific Postscript*, p. 126.
155. *S.V.*, IV, p. 313; *The Concept of Dread*, p. 38.
156. *S.V.*, IV, p. 381; *Ibid.*, p. 100.
157. *S.V.*, IV, p. 250; VII, pp. 172 ff.; *Philosophical Fragments*, p. 108; *Concluding Unscientific Postscript*, pp. 184-5.
158. *S.V.*, VII, pp. 168 and 176; *Concluding Unscientific Postscript*, pp. 180 and 188.
159. *S.V.*, VII, p. 430; *Ibid.*, p. 442.
160. *S.V.*, II, p. 201; *Either/Or*, II, p. 188.
161. *S.V.*, II, p. 194; *Ibid.*, pp. 181-2.
162. *S.V.*, XI, pp. 210 ff; *The Sickness unto Death*, pp. 162-3.
163. *Pap.*, X⁶ B 79.
164. *S.V.*, IX, p. 170; *Works of Love*, p. 174.
165. *S.V.*, IV, p. 377; *The Concept of Dread*, p. 97.
166. *S.V.*, IV, p. 377; *Ibid.*, p. 97.
167. *S.V.*, XIV, pp. 286 ff.; *Edifying Discourses* (Harpers), pp. 255 ff.
168. *Pap.*, XI² A 54.

169. *Pap.*, IV C 88.
170. *S.V.*, II, p. 158; *Either/Or*, II, p. 147.
171. *Pap.* X⁶ B 79.
172. *S.V.*, XIII, p. 533; *The Point of View*, p. 27.
173. *S.V.*, IV, pp. 373 ff.; *The Concept of Dread*, pp. 93-4.
174. *Pap.*, X¹ A 517.
175. *Pap.*, IX A 448.
176. *Pap.*, X⁶ B 127, p. 169.
177. *Pap.* VIII² B 58, 11.
178. *Pap.*, IX A 248.
179. *Pap.*, IX A 413, p. 241.
180. *S.V.*, XIII, p. 539; *The Point of View*, p. 38.
181. *S.V.*, XIII, p. 582; *Ibid.*, pp. 102-103.